Undoing Yourself
With
Energized Meditation
And
Other
Devices

FURTHER CONSPIRACIES?!

If you would like to read further on the New Age Conspiracy to elevate Human Consciousness on this Planet and elsewhere — don't simply ask your book dealer to order the following titles — **Demand that He/She do so!** They are:

The Cosmic Trigger by Robert Anton Wilson.
The New Inquisition by Robert Anton Wilson.
Prometheus Rising by Robert Anton Wilson.
Sex and Drugs by Robert Anton Wilson.
Wilhelm Reich In Hell by Robert Anton Wilson.
Coincidance by Robert Anton Wilson.
UnDoing Yourself With Energized Meditation And Other Devices by Christopher S. Hyatt, Ph.D. Introduced By Robert Anton Wilson.
Angel Tech A Modern Shaman's Guide To Reality Selection by Antero Alli. Introduced By Robert Anton Wilson.
An Interview With Israel Regardie — His Final Thoughts. Edited by Christopher S. Hyatt, Ph.D.
The Sapiens System: The Illuminati Conspiracy by Donald Holmes, M.D. Introduced by Robert Anton Wilson.
Zen Without Zen Masters by Camden Benares.
The DownSide Of Up by Marian Greenberg.
Monsters And Magical Sticks by Steven Heller, Ph.D.
The God-Spell —— Broken: A Study In Generic Humanity by Neil Freer.

A LAST MINUTE NOTICE

Timothy Leary, Ph.D. has just signed with Falcon Press for the following titles:

Exo-Psychology
Neuro-Politics
Intelligence Agents
What Does WoMan Want?
The Game Of Life

(Of course these books as well as many others are all by Falcon Press.)

UNDOING YOURSELF

WITH
ENERGIZED MEDITATION
AND
OTHER DEVICES

By

CHRISTOPHER S. HYATT

1987
FALCON PRESS
PHOENIX, ARIZONA 85012
U.S.A.

International Standard Book Number: 0-941404-06-4
Library of Congress Catalog Card Number: 82-83293

First Edition 1982
Second Printing 1986
(Revised) Third Printing 1987

Cover Design — Clara Cohan
Typesetting Design — Cate Mugasis

Falcon Press
3660 N. 3rd Street
Phoenix, Arizona 85012, U.S.A.

Manufactures in the United States of America

TABLE OF CONTENTS

Dedicated To My Beloved Teacher

Israel Regardie
(1907-1985)

ACKNOWLEDGEMENTS

The author is appreciative of the following individuals and sources:
Buddha
Zohar
G
IR
AC
TM
RAW
ARM
LMM
VLK
RAS
JSW
JMS
ELR
CCW
PVG
RARW
SG
KSM
LR
MRM
PZ
SS
CH

If you don't find yourself here be sure to let me know.

INTRODUCTION

by

Robert Anton Wilson, Ph.D.

The one sure way to make yourself unpopular in the United States these days is to mention the fact that Christianity and Democracy have been among the worst disasters to ever befall the human race. Nonetheless, as all students of history know, Christianity has been the bloodiest and most destructive religion in the long career of fanaticism on this planet; although Liberals and Rationalists keep reminding us of that tragic record of the Religion of Love, few of them have cared to observe or remember the data on warfare collected by Harvard sociologist, Prof. Pitrim Sorokin. In *Social and Cultural Dynamics*, and other works, Sorokin documents beyond all doubt that democratic nations have been involved in more imperialistic wars, and have fought them with greater ferocity, than any other kinds of governments, from the dawn of civilization to the present. Oriental despotisms, absolute monarchies, even modern fascist and communist nations have all had heinous records of tyranny and general human oppression, but collectively they have been much less aggressive and war-like than the democracies, from ancient Athens to modern America.

The blood-thirsty nature of Christianity and Democracy—which is obvious, psychologically, if one listens even for a few minutes to a typical speech by Rev. Jerry Falwell or his good friend Ronald Reagan—is, of course, based on arrogance, megalomania and a deep-rooted sense of total moral superiority to all non-Christian and non-Democratic peoples. But beyond that, the violent nature of Christian/Democratic countries is rooted in the singular delusion shared by both the Religion of Love and the Politics of Liberty. This delusion is the belief that human beings are born with some sort of metaphysical "free will" which makes them unique in the animal kingdom and only slightly less exalted than the gods themselves.

The "free will" fantasy is not a minor error, like thinking it is Tuesday when actually it is Wednesday. It is not even to be compared to a major intellectual blunder of the ordinary sort, like Marx's notion that once a totalitarian "worker's state" was created, it would then quickly and magically "wither away." It is even more nefarious and pernicious than the medieval lunacy that imagined witches everywhere and burned over 10,000,000 women at the stake on the basis of hysteria, superstition and the kind of hearsay and rumor that no modern court would permit to be entered as evidence. The "free will" delusion is much more serious than any of that. It is the kind of radical 180-degree reversal of reality that, once it enters a person's mind, guarantees that they will be incapable of understanding anything happening around them; they might as well be deaf, dumb, blind and wearing signs warning the world, "ULTIMATE DESTINA-TION: THE MADHOUSE."

I do not speak flippantly, nor do I mean to be understood as writing satire or polemic. The facts of modern biology and psychology have demonstrated clearly and conclusively that 99 percent of the human race is in a robotic or zombi-like state 99.99999 percent of the time. This does not refer to "other people." It refers to YOU AND ME. As the Firesign Theatre used to say, *We're all Bozos on this bus*. The best that can be said of any of us, usually, is that we have occasional moments of lucidity, but that can be said of any schizophrenic patient.

EAST, WEST AND THE MIDDLE

In the Orient, which has its own idiocies and superstitions, there has always been a singular sanity about the "free will" myth: virtually without exception, all the great Oriental philosophers have recognized that donkeys, grass-hoppers, dolphins, toads, humming-birds, dogs, chickens, tigers, sharks, gophers, spiders, chimpanzees, cobras, cows, lice, squid, deer, and humans are equally important, equally unimportant, equally empty, equally expressive of the "World Soul" or "Life Force." Buddhism, Vedanta and Taoism also recognize that each of these clever animals just mentioned, including the humans, have about equally as much "free will" as flowers, shrubs, rocks and viruses, and that the human delusion of being separate from and superior to the rest of the natural order is a kind of narcissistic self-hypnosis. Awakening from that egotistic trance is the major goal of every Oriental system of psychology.

Opposing this Oriental recognition of, and submission to, the order of things as they are, and yet opposing also the Christian and Democratic delusions of "free will" and "individual responsibility," there is the hidden tradition of Sufism in Islam and Hermeticism in Europe. This "occult" teaching recognizes that, although domesticated primates (humans) are born as mechanical as the wild primates (such as chimpanzees), there are techniques by which we can become *less* mechanical and approximate in daily and yearly increments toward freedom and responsibility.

These "spiritual" (neurological) techniques of Un-doing and re-robotizing oneself are, of course, of no interest in the Orient, where it is accepted that we are born robots and will die robots; and they are of even less interest in the Christian-Democratic cultures which assume that we are already free and responsible and do not have to work and work HARD to achieve even a small beginning of non-mechanical consciousness and non-robotic behavior.

The Orient forgives easily, because it does not expect robots to do anything else but what was programmed into them by the accidents of heredity and environment. The Christian and Democratic nations are so bloody-minded because they can forgive nothing, *blaming* every man and woman for whatever imprinted or conditioned behavior is locally Taboo. (This is why Nietzsche called Christianity "the Religion of Revenge" and Joyce described the Christian God as a Hanging Judge.) The Sufic and Hermetic traditions are almost Oriental in forgiving robots for being robots, but are far from sentimental about it. As one Sufi poet said:

> *The fool neither forgives nor forgets;*
> *The half-enlightened forgive and forget;*
> *The Sufi forgives but does not forget.*

That is, Sufism and other Hermetic traditions recognize that robots will behave like robots, and does not "blame" them, but it also does not forget, for a moment or even a nanosecond, that we are living in a robotic world—"an armed madhouse" in the metaphor of poet Allen Ginsberg. Those of this tradition know that when a man spouts Christian and Democratic verbalisms that does not mean he will act with brotherly love at all, at all; he will go on acting like a badly-wired robot in most cases.

Sufism is only the largest of several Near Eastern and European "mystic" movements which recognize the robotry of ordinary humanity but, unlike the Orient, attempt to Un-do and de-robotize those who have a dawning apprehension of their mechanical state and sincerely want to become less mechanical, as far as that is possible. I am not writing a recruiting manual for Sufism (which is doing quite well without my advertisements): I am merely using the Sufi school as one example of the tradition to which this marvelous book, *UNDOING YOURSELF*, belongs.

Most readers, if they have encountered such ideas at all, probably identify them with Gurdjieff and Ouspensky, two of the most talented expositors of a school of neo-Sufism which they peddled under the brand name of "Esoteric Christianity." The present book also owes a great deal to Aleister Crowley, who belonged to this tradition but sold his own brand of it under the label of Gnostic Magick. There is also a strong influence here of the bio-psychology of Wilhelm Reich; but all this tracing of "sources" is ultimately trivial. The importance of Christopher Hyatt's work is what you can get out of it and that depends entirely on what you put into it.

IT WORKS, IF YOU WORK

In my travels, I often encounter people who somehow have gotten the wild idea that I am the Head of the Illuminati (actually, I am at most a toe-nail) and who want me to explain the Secrets of High Magick to them. (Although it is hard to restrain my sense of humor at such times, I usually resist the temptation to tell them they can achieve Total Illumination by singing "Lucy in the Sky with Diamonds" in pig Latin while standing on their heads.) The questions I am asked most often, by those who can ask something more specific than "What is The Secret?" are almost always about Crowley's doctrine of the True Will. People tell me, most earnestly, that they have read ten or twenty or more of Crowley's books, and have read them many times, and still do not understand what "True Will" means.

As Gurdjieff would say, "What does this question signify? It signifies that these people are walking in their sleep and only dreaming they are awake. That is what this question signifies."

There is only one possible reason why people can read Crowley at length and *not* understand what True Will means. That reason seems incredible at first sight, but it is the only reason that can explain this astounding scotoma. The reason many readers of Crowley do not understand True Will is that these earnest students have never performed any of the exercizes that Crowley provides for those who sincerely want to de-robotize themselves and experience what is meant by True Will.

Shortly after my manual of de-mechanization exercizes, *Prometheus Rising*, was published, I was at a Cosmic Con with, among others, E.J. Gold of the Fake Sufi School. He told me that nobody would do any of the exercizes in my book, but I would still get lots of letters from people saying the book had "liberated" them. Since I sometimes think Sufis and even Fake Sufis are perhaps overly skeptical about humanity in its present evolutionary stage, I have made a point of asking people, when they praise that book in my presence, how many of the exercizes they've done.

Most people look faintly abashed and admit they have only done a "few" of the exercizes (which probably means they haven't done any). However, some people claim to have done all or most of the exercizes, and these people generally look so delighted about the matter that I tend to believe them. I therefore conclude that the Sufi and Gurdjieff traditions are wrong in saying that 999 out of 1000 will never work on the techniques of liberation. Actually, it appears to be only around 987 out of 1000 who prefer to talk about the work rather than doing it. At least 13 out of every 1000 will actually do the exercizes.

I have decided that one of the reasons that most readers of self-liberation books never even make the effort to liberate themselves is that reading the books is actually a kind of superstitious "magick ritual," which they think will have an effect with no other effort on their parts. The same sort of superstition leads others to think that peeking at the answers in the back of the book of logical puzzles is as beneficial as solving the puzzles for themselves; and there is even a text out now with the answers to Zen koans, as if the answers, and not the process of arriving at them, were the meaning of Zen.

Aside from such "symbolic magick" (as distinguished from real magick ritual, which is a type of Brain Change experiment), the main reason people prefer to read neurological exercizes rather than doing the exercizes is the dread and sheer horror which the word "work" invokes in most people. Some great teachers, especially Gurdjieff and Crowley, have literally frightened away thousands of would-be students by insisting on the necessity of HARD WORK (as I also frightened a lot of readers by using those words several times in this essay.)

Of course, there is a quite legitimate reason why the word "work" has such horrible conditioned associations for most people in the modern world. That reason is that most "work" in this age is stupid, monotonous, brain-rotting, irritating, usually pointless and basically consists of the agonizing process of being slowly bored to death over a period of about 40 to 45 years of drudgery; Marx was quite right in calling it "wage slavery." Most people know this, but are afraid to admit it, because to dislike "work" is regarded as a symptom of Communism or some other dreadful mental illness.

I recently heard a politician admit on BBC that the reason English workers are so notoriously "lazy" is that their jobs are so unspeakably sub-human and dull. "If I had to do that kind of work, I would call in sick as often as possible and goof off at every chance," he said flatly. Alas, I had tuned in late and never did catch this chap's name, which is a terrible misfortune for me, since I suspect he is the only Honest Politician in the world.

It is this universal but repressed hatred of "work" that causes almost everybody to despise and persecute the unemployed. Almost everybody envies the folks of the dole (on Welfare, as you say in The States) because almost everybody secretly wishes they could escape their own jobs and live without working.

It has taken me decades to understand this, because I am part of that very fortunate minority who work at jobs we actually enjoy. (It is hard to make me stop working, as my wife will assure you.) The minority who actually loves its work seems to be made up chiefly of the writers, dancers, actors and other artists, most scientists above the technician-troll level, computer freaks, and the righteous dope-dealers of California. Everybody else wishes they had the courage to go on the dole, but is ashamed of the stigma attached to being a non-worker, and resolves the tension by being as nasty as possible to the unemployed on every possible occasion.

HEY! CATCH THIS! A SECRET OF THE ILLUMINATI REVEALED!

Here I want to let you in on a real Secret of the Illuminati, one that has never been published before.

The so-called "work" involved in Brain Change is not like ordinary "work" at all. It is more like the creative ecstasy of the artist and scientist, once you really get involved in doing it. Most people are afraid of it only because they think "work" must be a curse and can't imagine that "work" can be fun.

So it is best not to think of Energized Meditation as "work" at all, at least as you have experienced "work" in most of the world today. It might be better and more accurate to consider the EM exercizes as "play" than as "work." Of course, play has its own rigours, and you do have to put energy into it to become a winner rather than a perpetual loser, but it is still entirely unlike the wage slavery that most people call "work." In fact, to be blunt about it, it is more like sex-play than any other kind of play because it definitely unleashes energies that have erotic as well as therapeutic side-effects. You are a dunce if you avoid it just because you think anything that needs effort must be "work" in the sense that people in factories and offices are suffering from the curse of "work" in our society.

Think of it more in terms of your favorite sport or recreation—fishing or bird-watching or softball or whatever you do with passion and just for the excitement of it. If that kind of thing should not be called "play," then I do not know what "play" means.

So when I wrote "Hard Work," I was just trying to jar you into actually paying attention for once. I really should have said, for accuracy, Hard Play.

The second part of this Secret of the Illuminati is what I have called elsewhere Wilson's 23rd Law. (Wilson's First Law, of course, is "Certitude belongs exclusively to those who only own one encyclopedia." Wilson's Second Law is the Snafu Principle described in ILLUMINATUS: "Communication is only possible between equals." All of Wilson's Laws will be published when the world is ready for the staggering revelations contained therein.)

Wilson's 23rd Law is

Do it every day

This is the most profound of all the Secrets of the Illuminati and I have often been warned that Terrible Consequences will ensue if I reveal it prematurely, but—what the hell, these are parlous times, friend, and this primitive planet needs all the Light that can be unleashed on its dark, superstitious mind. Let me repeat, since I am sure you didn't get it the first time:

Do it every day!

Have you ever wondered why Einstein became such a great physicist? It was because he loved the equations and concepts of mathematical physics so much that he "worked" on them—or played and tinkered with them—every day. That's why Otto von Klemper became such a great conductor: he loved Beethoven and Mozart and that crowd so much that he practised his music every day. It's why Babe Ruth became such a great ball-player: he loved the game so deeply that he was playing or rehearsing every day.

This rule also explains, incidentally, how people destroy themselves. Do you want to become a suicide (it's the fashionable thing in some circles, after all)? Practise being depressed, worried and resentful every day, and don't let anybody distract you with Energized Meditation or any other mind-change system. Do you want to land in jail on an assault and battery charge? Practise getting damned bloody angry every day. If you want to become paranoid, look carefully every day for evidence of treachery and duplicity around you. If your ambition is to die young, do the depression-worry-resentment system every day but center in especially on visualizing and worrying about every imaginable illness that might possibly inflict itself upon you.

(On the other hand, if you want to live as long as George Burns, "work hard" every day at being as cheerful and optimistic as he is.)

Almost anything is possible if you

DO IT EVERY DAY

Of course, this rule does not guarantee 100 percent results. Playing Chopin on the piano every day for 4 or 5 decades does not mean you will become as good as Van Cliburn; it merely means that you eventually will be a better piano player than anybody in your home state. Worrying every day does not absolutely guarantee a clinical depression or an early death, but after only a few years it does ensure you will be one of the three or four most miserable people in your neighborhood. Writing a sonnet every day for twenty years may not necessarily make you Shakespeare or Mrs. Browning, but it will make you the best poet for an area of about forty to fifty miles, probably. Doing Energized Meditation or similar excerizes does not mean you will be a Perfectly Enlightened Being or a Guru in a few years, just that you will be a great deal happier and a hell of a lot more perceptive, creative and "intuitive" than most people you'll meet in an average city.

There is a story that Bobbie Fisher, the chess champion, was once in a room with other chess masters when the conversation turned to the latest nuclear accident and the effects of the resultant fall-out. Fisher listened impatiently for a few minutes and then exclaimed irritably, "What the hell does that have to do with chess?" While I am not urging that you imitate that degree of monomania or obsession, there is a significant lesson in this tale. The reason Fisher became a champion is that he cared so much about chess that he did not even have to nag himself or remind himself to

do it every bloody day.

WARNING!
THREATS TO THE PRIMATE EGO ARE COMING!

Unfortunately—while the Energized Meditation system is fun, and erotic, and makes you "smarter" (in the sense of more aware of detail and complexity), and even jolts you out of total mammalian reflex behavior into something approximating in slow but definite increments toward that mystic "free will" Christians claim you were given at birth, and I recommend it heartily—I must admit that there are pages coming up shortly in this book that will probably make you extremely uncomfortable.

Dr. Hyatt is a rude, insulting and deliberately annoying writer. He does not soothe or pacify the reader with the Christian and Democratic mythology of our society by pretending that we are all free and rational people here. He insists on reminding us, every few pages, in the most blunt language possible, that most of us most of the time are conditioned chimpanzees in a cage.

Don't let it worry you too much.

The situation is this: there are mechanical systems operating throughout the domesticated primate (human) organism, each on different levels. For instance, as Bucky Fuller liked to say, you never sit down and ask how many hairs you should sprout on your head and body in the next week: that is one of the thousands of biological programs that operate entirely on mechanical circuitry. Except in various systems of yoga, you do not have much control over your breathing, either: that is also an auto-pilot. The digestive-excretive circuits also operate with a minimum of conscious attention or strategy, except when you need to find a public toilet and the bars are all closed. (Make a list of ten more programs that keep you alive and functioning, over which you have never had any conscious control. Be one of the 13 readers out of a thousand who actually do it before reading on.)

The reason that mystics and certain other psychologists are always "attacking" the ego is that the ego is the one mechanical circuit that suffers chronically from the illusion that it is non-mechanical and "free."

The ego and its delusions must be undermined—either attacked openly and bluntly, as in the Gurdjieff system and this book, or subverted more subtly and slowly, as in certain other systems—before any real progress can be made toward "liberation," "enlightenment," "finding IT," discovering the "True Will" in Crowley's sense, or whatever is your favorite term for becoming less robotic and more aware—less the computer and more the programmer of the computer—less the conditioned rat in the Behaviorist's maze and more the Beyond-Human that the Sufic-Hermetic traditions and Neitzsche have predicted.

The main reason you shouldn't be afraid of this attack on your precious little ego is that the ego is infinitely resourceful and finds ways to sneak back into its habitual mechanical trance no matter how many times you think you have Awakened once and for all. This is another Secret of the Illuminati and explains the great humility and the keen sense of humor of all the genuine Mages. In other words, if you think it is scarey to lose your precious primate ego abruptly and forever, don't worry about that; it is no more likely than becoming the world's greatest Rock star tomorrow morning. The only real way to get loose from mechanical ego trips is to learn

several ego-transcending games and then for twenty or forty years
or longer *DO THEM EVERY DAY*

   Before you put that much effort and time into it, you need
not worry that your wonderful, precious and totally marvelous Ego
will go away suddenly, it will merely get transformed a bit,
"enlarged" in perspective and "reduced" in conceit (a little), freed
from some of its more idiotic habits, and it will even pretend to go
away at times, but it will always come back and usually at the most
embarrassing times. It's easier to assassinate the President of the
United States than to kill your own ego.

   500 micrograms of pure Sandoz LSD will "destroy" the ego more
totally than any of the EM exercizes in this book—atom bomb it out
of existence, as it were. The results even in that case, as all old
acid-heads will assure you, are, however spectacular, always temporary.
As Dr. John Lilly wrote in *Programming and Metaprogramming in the
Human Biocomputer*, after a heavy trip on genuine laboratory Acid,

> For a time, the self then feels free, cleaned
> out. The strength gained can be immense; the
> energy freed is double . . . Humor appears in
> abundance, good humor . . . Beauty is enhanced,
> the bodily appearance becomes youthful . . .
> These positive effects can last as long as two to
> four weeks before reassertion of the old programs
> takes place.

   We are the products of mechanical genetic programs, mechanical
imprints and mechanical conditioning, just like the other animals.
The progress to post-animal, non-mechanical and trans-ego freedom
is often rapidly accelerated for a period, or several periods, of sudden
flash-like Awakenings and post-human perspectives, and I personally
suspect that is happening increasingly under the stress of our age of
terrorism and accelerated evolutionary change, but the ultimate
result of a true transcendence of robot consciousness is approached
in slow increments over years and decades. (Total "freedom" from
mechanism on all circuits seems impossible to me, in my current
level of ignorance. I don't think the organism would survive if most
of it did not remain a smooth-running and unconscious machine.)

   E.J. Gold of the Fake Sufi School, mentioned earlier, has a saying
to the effect that the attempt to achieve total Transcendence of

mechanical ego programs is as absurd as "sticking toothpicks between your eyelids to be sure you never go to sleep for a moment." There seem to be genuine biological reasons why we need to spend about one third of our lives asleep and a large part of the other two-thirds half-entranced by mechanical conditioned processes. The purpose of all schools of liberation is to wake up fully often enough to have some perspective outside the sleeping and conditioned ego states.

WHAT "IS" ALL THIS?

The great Dublin scientist and philosopher, de Selby, once took an empty jam jar and filled it with all the small cruddy items he could find around the house. The fuzz that accumulates on carpets, the dust on book shelves, bent paperclips, broken staples, the grunge from bathtub rings, grotty kitchen encrustations, nameless shards of forgotten plaster statues long broken, archeological excavations from the cellar, miscellaneous delvings in the rubbish bin, torn covers of match books scrawled with inscrutable phone numbers, even belly-button lint, all went in. This was a labour of some weeks, and when it was finished even de Selby himself could not remember or classify the total contents of the jar. He then selected a statistical universe of 123 Dubliners and 246 visitors form England or the Continent just off the Dun Laoghaire ferry and asked each to guess what the jar contained.

77.6 percent of the sample answered at once, "Oh, I know, it is ——" and then made some wild guess. (The most common guess, given by 54.3 percent, was that it "was" the stuff mixed into the curry sauce in Pakistani restaurants. Others commonly said it "was" uranium ore, wood cement and tree bark.)

Of the 22.4 percent who did not guess what it "was," 83.5 percent immediately asked the directions to Clontarf Castle and presumably did not want to guess because they were in hurry to catch the evening Musical show.

De Selby concluded that most Europeans, at this stage of evolution, believe that everything and anything can meaningfully be described in a simple proposition in the form, "This is a thingamajig."

I believe, on the basis of experience, that similar results would be found in an American sample of the same size. We are still haunted by the ghost of Aristotle, the bloke who first tried to describe and explain the whole universe in permutations of sentences having the form, This is a Y, All Z are Y, Some Y are X, therefore some Z are X. Most people, and especially most politicians and clergymen, remain firmly convinced that anything and everything can be meaningfully discussed in that Aristotelian manner—or as Ernest Fenollosa once said, Western culture thinks that "A ring-tailed baboon is not a Constitutional Assembly" is one of the two types of meaningful statements (the other being "The U.S. Congress and U.K. Parliament are Constitutional Assemblies.")

From the point of view of current science, c. 1980-87, there appear to be two things wrong with this Aristotelian mind-set. In the first place, scientific models are not expressed in this metaphor of identity (A is a B) but in the functional language of relationships (When A moves an increment of x in any dimension, B will move an increment of y in some other dimension.) The latter type of functional statement allows for scientific predictions, which can be partially verified or totally refuted by experience and experiment; the former, Aristotelian type of is-ness statement leads only to verbal argument.

The second objection to Aristotelian A is a B statements is that they appear totally contradicted by neurology and experiments with instruments. Neurologically, we never know what A "is," but what it appears to our senses and brain. The senses pick up some (not all) the signals of the space-time event and the brain edits and orchestrates these signals into some familiar Gestalt. (This seems to be how de Selby's subjects edited and orchestrated a jar full of junk into Pakistani sauce or uranium ore.) Instrumentally, the same editing goes on. An instrument does not tell us what A "is" but what class of signals from A that particular instrument can measure. A voltmeter tells us nothing about the temperature of A, a thermometer tells us nothing about the height of A, a ruler or scale tells us nothing about the molecular structure of A, etc.—each instrument creates its own gloss or reality-tunnel, just as our inner instruments (brain and perceptors) create a gloss or reality-tunnel. To speak accurately, we should never say "This 'is' an A," but, rather, "This seems to fit the category of A in my system of glossing or in this instrument's reality-tunnel."

Does this sound like pedantry or unnecessary hair-splitting? Consider for a moment the human suffering and social catastrophes that have been unleashed in various times and places by such statements as "Miss Jones is a witch," "Mr. Smith is a homosexual," "Mr. Goldberg is a Jew," "This book is heretical," "This painting or photo is pornography." If you think about this deeply enough, it might almost appear that the Catholic witch-hunts, most idiotic censorship, Hitler's annihilation camps and quite a few other historical horrors never would have happened if we had no words for "is" in our languages, or if we remembered that "is" always functions as a metaphor.

Most of the guilt and "chronic low-grade emergency" (as Fritz Perls called it) which keeps you from realizing your full potential can usually be traced to some sentence having the form "I am a B" in which B equals roughly "no-good shit." That sentence got conditioned into you when you were very young and you may not think it consciously any more, or you may well think it and even say it aloud frequently, but if you feel basically unhappy with your life some such sentence exists somewhere in your brain.

Even is-ness sentences that seem factual contain dangers due to the mechanical-conditioned level of most human consciousness on this planet at this time. "He is a homosexual" may appear a safe remark when heard in a Group Encounter session, or at a San Francisco cocktail party, but in the Bible Belt, "homosexual" contains the conditioned association of "sinner" and particularly nefarious "sinner" at that, and it is not unknown for violence or even murder to result from this is-ness sentence, just as "Jew" seems to be a neutral label for one of three major religions of the West but in Nazi Germany signified somebody subject to arrest, slave labor and eventual execution.

I read recently in a science-fiction fan magazine, "The Irish really are disgusting." Leaving aside my own mechanical prejudices (as a person of partially Irish genetic structure who lives by preference in Ireland) the most fascinating thing about this is-ness statement seems to me that it occurred in a publication where one would never see such semantically isomorphic statements as "The Jews really are sub-human" or "Women really are inferior to men."

To quote Mr. G. again, "What does this signify? It signifies that most people are walking in their sleep and dreaming they are awake." That is, certain historically infamous types of racial or sexual stereotypes have become unfashionable and virtually Taboo in "educated" circles, but the mechanical conditioned reactions underlying such stereotypes still exist, the machine is still asleep, in Gurdjieff's terms, so people who would not stereotype Jews see nothing inconsistent in stereotyping the Irish or the Poles or some other group. In a mechanical or primitive stage of evolution, this cannot be considered surprising.

What does still surprise me (occasionally) is that people who can see this mechanical level of functioning in others can remain blissfully oblivious of the same mechanisms in themselves.

One way to understand Energized Meditation, and simultaneously grasp the significance of what I have just been saying about Aristotelian habits, is to apply mathematical subscripts to significant nouns in the manner urged by the semanticist, Alfred Korzybski. For instance, the Nazi mentality consists of something like

$$Jew_1 = Jew_2 = Jew_3 = Jew_4 \text{ etc.}$$

Now this is obviously false to sensory-sensual space-time experience. In sensory-sensual space-time experience—or what we ordinarily call "reality" if we haven't been ruined by philosophy courses—every Jew we meet is a specific event in the space-time continuum. The first may be a poet, the second an actress, the third a grocer, etc. if we place this group in the gloss of category-by-occupation. Put them in the category of good looks, and the first may seem as handsome as Paul Newman, the second as unhandsome as Edward G. Robinson, the third as cute as Barbra Streisand, etc. Put them in any other grid, and differences still emerge, just as there are no two leaves on an oak tree that are exactly the same in all respects.

Don't go back to sleep yet; hang in there a moment. We are not preaching a sermon on "tolerance" like a 1950s Hollywood movie. We are just using anti-semitism as an example of a mechanical mental set that illuminates many, many other mechanical mental sets that you are going to have to recognize in yourself if Energized Meditation is to do you any good.

For instance, at the beginning, for the shock effect, I said some critical things about Christianity and Democracy. If you drew the conclusion that I dislike *all* aspects of Christian and Democratic society, you had a mechanical "is" somewhere in your evaluations. In fact, I would much rather live in Christian Democratic nations, for all their faults, than in any of the Moslem Fundamentalist nations or Buddhist nations, and I would rather be gored by a rhinoceros than try to live in a Marxist nation. As for fascist nations, whether I tried to cope or not, I rather suspect they would shoot me in a few months, if not in the first week.

If the Nazi mentality acts "as if" Jew_n = Jew_k or any Jew is "the same" as any other Jew, people who seem a lot more sophisticated often act "as if" any Rock music = any other Rock music (it "is" all equally wonderful or equally "barbarous"), or any science fiction novel = any other science fiction novel (the book critics in *Time* seem to have that mechanical conditioned reflex), or "all television should be abolished" (there was a book on that subject recently, in which the author seriously seemed to have the Nazi-like hallucination that TV $show_n$ = TV $show_k$), or any cop = any other cop, or any fast food place is as "bad" as any other fast food place, etc.

Mechanical reactions are the statistical norm; full conscious attention remains very rare. (That's why one Zen Master always gave the answer "Attention!" when he was asked what Zen "is.") We started from that unChristian and unDemocratic premise and we have worked our way back to it by a circuitous route, but now perhaps we can see more clearly what this mechanical A=B hypnosis does to us.

We have been using examples of difference between elements of the "same" group, but no element remains unchanged in time. Consider yourself as an element, X, in the group "humanity." It should be obvious that

$$X_{1987} \text{ is } not \text{ } X_{1976}$$

You have changed quite a bit in the last ten years, have you not? If people weren't in the habit of calling you by the same name, you might not even "believe" that the You of today "really is" in some sense the You of 1976. In fact, if you can forget your name for a few moments, the entity or more precisely the space-time event called You obviously was changing, sometimes faster and sometimes more slowly all through the decade. If you are more than 20 years old, just think of how absurd it would be to claim that the You of 1986 "really is" the You of 1966 . . .

Think about this seriously. It would be a damned good idea, right now, to make a list of ten important changes that have occurred in "You" since 1966 and ten changes since 1976. Is it too much trouble to get a paper and pen? Well, at least make a list in your head. Can you even visualize what you looked like and dressed like in 1966? Really think hard about some of the other changes in You over 20 years.

Now, to understand what this book can do for you, try to apply this awareness on a smaller time-scale. Is it possible that You$_{last\ week}$ "really is" in every respect You$_{this\ week}$? Alas, this may almost seem possible, but it is not strictly true unless you have died and they pickled you in formaldehyde.

Think, really, about the changes in "You" in one week. How many more changes could have occurred in that week, if You did not have the illusion that You are a finished product and not a Work in Progress?

Keep at it. Think seriously about whether it is strictly and totally true that You$_{yesterday}$ really is You$_{today}$.

When you get to the point of understanding that You$_{one\ second\ ago}$ is not strictly You$_{right\ here\ and\ now}$, then you are ready to begin to understand what Christopher Hyatt is offering you in this book and how you can *use* it.

Howth, Ireland
17 November 1986

INTRODUCTION

by

Israel Regardie

Systems of meditation come and go — and have since time immemorial. But somehow meditation is more popular to-day and I fancy practised by more people than ever before in the world's history. My contention is that this is largely due to the psychedelic movement initiated by Aldous Huxley's *Doors of Perception* and the fantastically pioneering work of **Timothy Leary**. Posterity, I am certain will have a finer appreciation of what he has contributed to this world than we have today.

Meditation is meditation. But there are innumerable techniques for achieving the proper results. One of the most dynamic that has appeared in recent years is not Transcendental Meditation by the grinning-giggling Monkey faced guru, though perhaps this is the most popular, but the so-called chaotic meditation of Bhagwan Shree Rajneesh. This is the one that really comes nearest to the vital and powerful method described by our author Christopher S. Hyatt. Without equivocation, it can truthfully be stated that this method is by far and away about the best method I have encountered in all my years in both psychotherapy and in the occult world.

As Alan Watts pointed out a long time ago, most Western psychotherapy is fundamentally metaphysical—that is it is essentially conceptual and verbal. Whereas Eastern "psychotherapy" is more realistically and somatically oriented - *viz* Yoga in all its facets and branches. To this extent the latter is more holistic than the metaphysical approach of the West. (An unusual and unexpected dichotomy that was first indicated by Alan Watts.) Christopher Hyatt's work is the closest technique to this model.

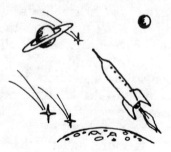

The author has been, amongst many other things, a classical psychologist, a practitioner of Reichian therapy, and a 20 year student of the occult. From years of clinical experience he has distilled the essence of his experience in a most astute and shocking manner. In a fantastically penetrating, humorous and insightful fashion he has also distilled the essential factor in Zen meditative techniques. The result is a meditative system that is wholly unlike any other. Even the design of the book and the way it is presented suggests the purpose of the Great Work. As such it can be altogether recommended to those who have tried all other systems of meditation and found them wanting; their failure can be compensated for and overcome by the use of this extraordinary dynamic approach.

I recommend it enthusiastically and without any reservation whatsoever. In fact I am excited and exhilarated by its discovery.

It should prove to be the answer to the frustration felt by the thousands and more who have tried the other systems and failed. However, I do warn the reader, if you don't really want to change, don't take this book seriously.

Israel Regardie
March 11, 1982
SOMEWHERE HAVING FUN

IS THERE ANYTHING NEW UNDER THE SUN?
Or The Key To Uncoding The Purpose Of This Book

by

Christopher S. Hyatt, Ph.D.
and Baron Peter von Gundlach

It has been four years since *Undoing Yourself* was released and approximately two years since the first edition was sold out. The book was not reissued until now because I was in a moral dilemma concerning the message contained in this work.

It is suggestive as well, that agents in both Israel and Germany requested copies of this book for possible translation. However, after further reading, both withdrew their requests. This also contributed to my hesitance to re-publish the work.

Many dear friends and associates made suggestions as to what I should do regarding the criticisms levelled at this book. I listened to all that was said and waited until the right moment, which is now, to answer both the attacks and the compliments.

The primary attack came from the intellectual community. This of course is to be expected. Their attitude was one of abhorrence that such a work could be published at all. Specifically, they felt that the book was "disgusting" irrelevant and down right "stupid."

What they found disgusting, was the "irrelevant" pictures, the "provocative and hostile" writing style and the "stupid" content. Some of these critics simply felt pity, since they assumed the author was "justly" uneducated. Others were shocked at the revelation that the author held three advanced degrees and was finishing a fourth. Some suggested that the meditation technique ("which might be the only thing of value") be published by itself and the rest buried somewhere out of smell and sight.

I pondered this and said no! . I then asked myself what was so terrible about this book? The answer I found was that it attacked the channelization process of the biological imperative, (those of nesting, digesting and congesting, or to say it more correctly, housing, eating, and making babies) and that it exposed the hypocrisy that exists between what the intellect says and what the body does. That is, it challenged the so-called idealism, the hypocritical screen, between ideas and actions, but more importantly it elevated biology over culture.

As the title of this book implies *Undoing Yourself With Energized Meditation and Other Devices* is a workbook of emancipation and not a collection of ideas to be perused by smug dilettantes. These critics, who profit from the system they endorse, protect and maintain, which even they admit feeds on the surpluses of social inequities, are simultaneously condemning it in lecture and writing as they blissfully enjoy its fruits. These are the most vociferous assailants of this book. Why?

The answer is simple. This is a book on psycho-social-biology, (or more correctly a spiritual-biology) something which most intellectuals and people in general find abhorrent, for this topic exposes the schizoid foundations of their reality set. Yes, this book is really a disguised text on the fundamental motivation of human existence on this planet. In other words, this book is about the bio-survival of the species and its most observable result—the genetic-class struggle. This book is about power and freedom, something which we all desire, and the lies and "stories" which preempt and hoard the truth about how to use this bio-spiritual imperative successfully, profitably and "decently". How is this deception accomplished? And more importantly by WHO?

THE MALADAPTIVE FALLACY
The What and The Who of it!

The maladaptive fallacy is based on the assumption that man's nature is inherently flawed. What does this mean? *Miss Man aged Man* has decided through aeons of self-reflection that what the observer observes (man) is in fact — "No-Dam-Good." This is the indictment — the moral accusation. The followers of this verdict believe that the proof of this is man's own behavior, i.e., wars, dis-obedience to God, class struggle, and an array of similar stupidities. On the other hand, the small voice of his defense whispers that man has also co-operated with the evolutionary imperative for his enlightened self-interest. Some examples are charity, medicine, science, heroism, etc. Which ever tunnel reality they choose to focus on, both are inappropriate since it has been assumed that man is a completed product. What both sides do not see is that mankind is nothing but the result of the trial and error (also known as trial and success) factor of a great bio-spiritual experiment. The problem lies in the fact that "trial and error" is the culture that is regarded as more sacrosant than the biology which forms its base.

The Relatives of Man

The last one hundred years has brought us the theory of relativity — ironically interpreted and used as an absolute. Relativity theory may have done wonders for physics and the other sciences, but it has been mis-used almost everywhere else. People invoke Einstein, the absolute authority, as a defense for their most stupid and ignorant theories and mis-representations of facts. Their logic, if you can call it that goes something like this. "I invoke the theory of relativity, by the authority of Einstein, to prove that my authority, (and ideas) are as equally valid as anyone else's." Most of them never heard of testing their theories in the lab. This sort of non-sense, takes the place of learning and effort. The fortunate thing about this process, however, is that it is a reflection of the rebellion against blind authority, that is authority for authority's sake. Unfortunately, the rebels often justify the need for "more" irrational authority, since their—opinions often lack the stuff of which planets are made—they simply want to be the boss. Einstein, I believe would be absolutely appalled by the mis-use of his ideas found in both the soft sciences and the occult. All opinions are not equal. All tunnel realities are not equal, for equality would obviate the necessity for our diversity.

Ideas must be left in the form of working hypotheses open to argument, the approximation of the truth found by the process of experimentation. Man must be left free to conduct his experiments unhampered by the mere conventions of culture.

As we obtain more knowledge, our need to hide the apparent injustice of creation in flowery ideas and terms will dissolve into a spiritual biology, something other than the common clap-trap of those who refuse the eye of clarity. While the present author is also guilty of clap-trap, he does take immense pride in the fact, that on occasion, he is aware of his right hand pulling the wool over his left eye.

DEATH HAS BEEN CONQUERED! NOW WHAT?
(Sir! In what newspaper did you read that?)
(Hey! I didn't read it — I thought it! Aren't Thoughts Reality?)
(Answer! It depends on who is doing the thinking
and how much ability they have to make it real.)
FUTANT-MUTANTS LIKE IDEAS THAT WORK!

When death is conquered then what? Why do I ask this question at this point of the discourse? The answer! Most of the clap-trap surrounds our own sense of impermenance. We explain ourselves away, with words of Karma, reincarnation, etc., which for the life of me, (this life that is) the time would better be spent in the laboratory of life seeking results. In other words let God worry about His experiments, and you worry about your own! Theories about what God is doing and why, are nothing but an ointment heated by the frustration of our helplessness in accepting our present fate — FRUSTRATION & DEATH!

A solution to this struggle is simply to locate your part of the drama and fulfill it. That is find your true will and follow it to the end. Struggle is the crux of life. However, do not despair at this word, for it is through this almost never-ending parade of frustration, that the true Man emerges as Hero. While some of you may not think so, cessation from struggle is death. The Buddha said, "if it doesn't kill you, it makes you stronger." Did he say that?

Why do you think man is always facing a new problem? Man is a problem-solver, this is his life's blood, his holiness if you would. No other animal is in an almost continuous state of dissatisfaction, no matter how much and how great his accomplishments. There will be no final rest from this process, no utopia, thank God, for then it would be over once and for all. Challenge is always on the horizon, and it is built into our DNA, or biology. Even Buddha struggled to stop struggling, and when he accomplished that he continued to struggle to enlighten the world.

When death is conquered, we will still require the struggle, for even our hope for freedom from struggle, is a struggle, (it often terrifies me, that most writers forget that the category includes itself). For example, is the idea of tunnel reality, a tunnel reality, or is it a meta-tunnel reality, etc. Labelling something or a process does not always free one from its effects. We are all on the front lines of life and death. Take it very seriously because it is happening right now in front of and in you. But do not forget to laugh, lest you miss the point.

THE SPECIFICS

Let us begin with nesting (housing). In all instances, a place to live, a shelter is a biological essential, be it a mansion, cave, tree, or a space on the ground. A shelter requires a site. Space or location for the shelter necessitates territory. Thus, the biological essential, shelter, requires territory. As space begins with the body, its extension symbolized by shelter and territory, is an expansion of the body boundary. Hence tactileness; our perceptions of heat and cold, wet and dry, privacy and exposure or, in other words, pain and pleasure. The skin is the psycho-physical barrier between our personal and public selves. The skin, if you would, is the sensate membrane of how we know who, what and where we are, and what we are doing. The body, the skin, represents both our individuality which we cherish, and at the same time our vulnerabilty which we abhor.

Thus public exposure regardless of form is always a threat, be it spatial or psychological. In other words, we are always scared of each other.

As long as our biology demands our survival, our primary mode of operation is fear. However, we are deliberately made unaware of this, or told that our anxieties are abnormal. In fact our anxieties are the most normal things about us and are the fuel and engine from which society and culture are built. We have been told to reject our biology, particularly by those who demand more territory for their own biological safety. ("Paranoia will destroy ya.")

Society is structured in order to implement and exploit the product of the "maladaptive fallacy." The maladaptive fallacy is the assumption that man is flawed and evil. In order to correct our "pathology" we have military, police, psychologists, sociologists, university professors, physicians, priests, politicians and their ilk whose "soul" purpose is to mold us into productive agents for their employment, allowing us to accumulate possessions which will be re-distributed through acts of violence and war.

In other words the "original sin" is nothing but the "original lie". Taking the byte from the Apple of the Tree of Knowledge at the suggestion of the Serpent of the DNA, was a window of opportunity offered to mankind to accept his true nature — that of the experimenter. That this has been historically mis-represented as anathema to spirituality was the first great lie and subversion of our Godly or true purpose of existence. It precipitated our expulsion from our natal territory, the Garden of Eden — our biology. In other words, what has been called the lowly in us is actually the exalted. Our territoriality or our biology is not the cause of our misery, it is the rejection and denial of it which therefore results in its perverted and dangerous expression. The founding fathers of America, an "occult group", was deeply aware of this and tried to make allowances for our most primary and basic genetic tendencies.

What has been labelled our animal nature is in reality the image of God in which we were created. Our natural desire for terror—Tory has brought about not only wars through its perversion, but has brought about every major and minor convenience; medical and technological breakthroughs from penicillin to spaceships. These discoveries are designed to help us improve our nesting, digesting and congesting.

Anxiety then is a normal and biological necessity. Anxiety is always related to territory (our location in space-time.) It is of more than passing interest to note that the population of mental institutions is lowest from the transitions of peace to war and of war to peace. That is, anxiety which is based on territory, results in less mental disturbance during territorial shifts. Institutionalization arises during periods of non-territorial shifts or more correctly during territorial-anxietal stasis.

The desire and concern for territory is a primary and functional biological need hard wired into the neuro-genetic system. The channelization of this need, i.e. how it is expressed, is the function of culture, which is nothing more than biology's interaction with geography thus forming a bio-culture feedback loop which feeds on and digests itself. Thus, the primacy of HOW (culture) is substituted for the primacy of WHAT and WHY (territory and biologic-motivation).

Therefore our measure of worth is based on the value, size, and location of our monuments, edifices and estates, and rituals (such as weddings, funerals, and confirmations) which we can identify as our personal territory or genetic mandate. This is our zone of safety, which is only natural and proper. What is not natural and proper is that we are told that we should feel guilty for this desire, thus forcing us to become as schizoid as our mentors. Wars therefore are not a result of territoriality, but a cause of dis-placed motivation. Instead of territoriality being our great despair, it is in fact our great hope. The reader may ask, then, why do we find a book of psycho-social biology on bookshelves which are labelled occult or meditation? The answer is simple. Occult means hidden. Something which is hidden, once exposed, is no longer occult. Like lifting up a rock. What was under the rock was occult, until someone had the courage or curiosity to pick it up. What is still occult for most of us is the neuro-biological connection. Our neuro-biology is our absolute. How we channel this neuro-biology is our relativism. Thus the "occult" is that *biology and anatomy is destiny*, in that order. That is to say, WHAT we do is determined, HOW we do it is relative. We all are born, we all eat, groom, sleep, have sex, require shelter, etc. How we do this determines our class in the structure of society, which is based on presently unalterable biological imperatives.

In conclusion of this section the biological is the absolute and the cultural is the relative. We have been taught this fundamental truth in reverse, bacteria is for culture, rather than culture is for bacteria. We revere the cultural and loath the biological. This is both a denial of "God" and the source of our potential destruction.

Part II
DIGESTING

When we think of digestion the first thing that comes to mind is the consumption of food, i.e. that which feeds and nourishes us. Consumption takes place before digestion and is involved with an entire cycle of influence and effluence (consumption, digestion, and elimination).

Digestion in and of itself is a key, for it tells us that the things of value are automatically taken out by the bodily process and the "offal" is eliminated. This natural model must then take the place of our cultural process of consumption, digestion and elimination for its purpose is not to eliminate the unnecessary but to sell it.

A story told to us about a study in animal husbandry may help to make the point clearer. Swine were placed in three tiers of cages, where the pigs in the top cage were fed fresh food, the pigs in the lower cages ate the postdigested excretions of their upper neighbors. The ones that increased their weight most for the volume of substance consumed were those in the middle cages. The conclusions were that those on the top ate well but did not gain as much weight as the ones in the middle. The ones on the bottom faired the worst, though all survived.

This provides an interesting model for our cultural "imperative." The middle class takes the refined elements of the wealthy, i.e. products — consumes and over-eats, then distorts and destroys the idea which created the product, and feeds the result (offal) to the lower classes, while at the same time deploring their lowly condition. In other words, ideas and risk create products which are consumed by the middle class in their attempt to mimic the higher classes.

This process of vulgarization is paid for by the lower class, which is eternally maintained by the middle classes cult of conformity. The lower classes, the final consumer on the food chain, are also the criminals from which the middle class primarily demands to be protected by the existing machinery of suppression. In other words, the criminal class, (excluding "white collar criminals") consisting primarily of the lower classes and minorities, is both created and used by the other classes as justification to protect their perverted and excessive expectations. Again it is important to remember that it is not our biology which is to blame, but rather the lie surrounding it.

It is of great interest to note that in Europe there is conscious recognition of the class struggle. In America we insulate ourselves from this dynamic. We shake our head yes to the pain and misery of the less fortunate, while we feather our nests with more and more symbols which serve to reassure us that we have elevated ourselves. The lower classes, like the pigs on the lowest tier, consume what is discarded. Finally, in America the struggle is not really between the lower classes and the upper classes, for they are too far apart. The struggle here is between the middle classes and the lower classes.

Part III
THE REPRODUCTION BIAS — CONGESTION
The Tree of Life as the Genetic Chain
The Neuro-Politics of Obsolescence

The reproduction bias simply means that the majority of our time and resources is spent on re-assuring the survival of the species. These are called reproduction strategies. The important point is that, while reproduction is in itself absolute, the strategies are relative, and thus open to change. The bias part of the phrase relates to the *absolutizing* of the relative, a process which the class struggle not only creates but demands. That is we require consumers, upwardly mobile ones, as well as the lower classes who consume the left-over by-product "offal" of the reproduction bias.

Reproduction is the model of perpetual obsolescence and replacement. It is also a form of imagined personal immortality. Reproduction, however, in its grossest sense is entirely impersonal. There is nothing new or unique about having offspring (DNA coils). What is unique in terms of our experience is the territoriality engendered by having offspring. That is they are a part of our body, yet no human invented DNA, nor did any human create the sperm and egg which combined to create a new replacement.

In this sense our territorial imperative serves to create a bond. Like everything in the world we too are obsolete, nothing is built to last forever.

We are trapped in the model of renewal which we apply to most every facet of our existence. This structures our hierarchy of priorities. Consequently we incorporate aspects of impermanence into the products we build and into the lives we lead. On the other hand we also have the paradox of surrounding ourselves with non-functional objects which represent our wish for permanence such as statues, icons, tomb stones, antique furniture, etc. We do not accept our finiteness with humility. Our daily attitudes towards most relationships and objects are *as if* we might last forever. The consequence of this is wasteful redundancy in every aspect of our lives, be it economic or psychic. We work all of our lives to re-produce labor saving devices. This play on the words "labor" and "reproduction" is no accident.

The child or baby, as we begin to "humanize" our discussion, is an exercise in labor of both male and female. The pain of labor in western culture is no accident either. Pain and struggle stimulates a sense of ownership. When we struggle for something we feel we own it. The division of labor between male and female in regards to off-spring production and rearing in and of itself creates a dynamic of conflict between the now new mother and father. By mystifying the entire birth process we provide an elevated meaning which it neither requires nor deserves. This is the process of "*absolutizing* the relative and *relativizing* the absolute."

The agenda of reproduction for the female is bio-survival security, a guaranteed sanctuary (nest) and a source of income, assured by the male authorities. This agenda is being modified by the new awareness of the women's liberation movement. The emerging matriarchy is attempting to address this issue from a healthier perspective. It suggests the promising beginnings of human liberation, again not from our biology, but from our distortions of it. Its principle slogan being, "that society, i.e. the patriarchy, no longer owns my body." Unfortunately, the consensual cultural program is not impressed, nor has it been significantly altered by this new paradigm. The male justification for the patriarchy is due to the unconscious recognition of his biological expendability as can be easily observed in other species. This attitude of male redundancy prevents women from risking death in most cultures by fighting wars. Women then are protected in many other ways as well, not because they are better, or loved, but because they are believed as essential for the nurturance of the offspring (the new consumer).

An obvious example can be demonstrated by society's attitude toward rape victims. The woman is frequently seen as the culprit. The paradox of both protecting the female, as the potential matrix of birth and the degrading attitudes expressed by the patriarchy is a consequence of the subtle view that all humans of the middle and lower classes are chattel, i.e. consumers (part of the food chain). Though democracy offers the illusion of individual participation or effect on the whole, in reality it presents an environment of economic and psychic serfdom. A good mantram upon awakening is to repeat three times, "Serfs Up." P.S. "And don't forget the bored."

To return to the main point, any new male or representative of society for that matter can take the place of the genetic father after fertilization. The female's love for the male must be transferred to the developing baby. After birth, the male is primarily unnecessary except as a facilitator of goods and services. This is a cultural fact and not a biological one. In other words there is nothing wrong with a love shift, what is disturbing is that we are not informed of the natural processes of birth, death and life in general. Biology again has been exploited to serve certain cultural distortions — "Trials and Errors."

From the male point of view, the biological reward for reproduction is a pat on the back for having virile sperm and the identification with his genetic offspring. Again the process is personalized beyond the point of necessity simply to satisfy the pride of possession. Time is spent in identifying those physical and character qualities of the offspring which resemble those of the parents. Identifying common genetic characteristics of the infant is done more for the re-assurance of the male, for he can never really know if the child is his in fact. This provides an edge for the female in any future negotiations with her husband. Possession is 9 tenths of the law. Thus the offspring is viewed by both the parents and the courts as belonging to the female. Judicial preference for child custody by the mother is proof of the matter.

Will not any set of teats do for nurturing the child, just as will not any sperm do for the fertilization of the egg? The answer is both yes and no. Arguments can be had for either side of the issue. However, in the long run it does not matter. What is of importance is the child, for it assures the continuation of the race and a specific set of selfish genes. Again, biological necessity cannot be blamed for how any particular culture channelizes this force. What can be blamed is elevating the *relativism* of culture over the *absolutism* of biology. Which is really more sacred?

SOLUTIONS

The major premise in this paper is that biology is primary to culture, and that the problems assumed to be caused by biology are a result of biology's distortion by culture. The first general solution is the daily remembering that culture is relative. The second is that territoriality is not destructive in itself and contributes directly to the evolutionary process. Thus any attempt to modify territoriality by governmental intervention as in communism, is destructive to life, liberty and the pursuit of happiness. The U.S. constitution and the Bill of Rights is a biological and spiritual document. Additionally the hypocrisy created by the non-gnostic Christian, non-Sufi

Moslem and non Kabbalistic Jewish paradigms are also destructive to the growth and evolution of the species. Original sin is the original lie. Nothing more, nothing less.

Leaving the general to focus on the particular we offer some creative and interesting solutions to counter the mal-adaptive fallacy.

Specifically, to deal with space and housing we present the idea of the Shalhome which is a shelter that can be built for between $5.00 and $20.00 a square foot. This is housing both beautiful and functional which can be constructed using the most simple tools and requiring little or no skill. How does this shelter deal with the idea of nesting? Being made of concrete and steel it requires little up-keep and maintenance. Since the Shalhome is available to more people there would be less hostile struggle over territory.

Why are banks, planning committees, and husbands and wives opposed to alternative housing? Culture and habit have dictated zoning and sub-division restrictions which have imposed on us human packaging systems in the form of "boxes." A home does not have to be a box, yet the *absolutizing of the relative*, creates the illusion that boxes and homes are co-extensive. This means when we say shelter, home, etc., we automatically "see" boxes. The Shalhome is circular, thus many would not accept it as a home, since box is equal to home. The word is not the object, nor is necessity the form (i.e. necessity is shelter, the form is the box).

Having built-in furniture, there is no burden (re-decoration syndrome) to replace obsolete and no longer fashionable appointments. Following the design format the form of the structure makes it indistinguishable in terms of class identification. The only differences are size, contents and location. The Shalhome can function as an energy conversion matrix which can employ a broader range of options for heating and cooling. Inexpensive, functional and beautiful shelter encourages pride of ownership which decreases crime. Community participation is an important part in its creation. In other words everyone can have their own territory and shelter for a minimal cost. Instead of homes which cost 65$ plus a square foot, we have a home for no-more than $20.00 a square foot and frequently less.

While we are completely aware that this example does not solve all the distortions of the territorial instinct, we do believe that it offers an option to those who do not want to spend the rest of their lives working as serfs for the bankers and real estate speculators.

The true ideal of democracy is not practiced anywhere in the

world today. As it is practiced, it is divorced from its roots, the intelligence and spirit of the people. Most of us have little or no knowledge of the candidates that represent us. This is reflected by apathy at the polls. We appear to be willing to pay the price to have others make our critical decisions for us.

In a bi-partisan political system the choices are indistinguishable, both in the poverty of new ideas and the similarity of the professional leader complex. The excessive costs of surrogate management are due to an imperfect mechanism of monitoring and controlling the politician's conflict between his/her desire for personal aggrandizement and public duty. To compound the flaws, politicians as our representatives, frequently band together in special interest groups, promoting objectives and agendas which are contrary to the best interests of the people. Election and re-election both imply compromises to the point where no-one is served except those who can wield the most money.

In other words politics should not be an occupation, since the present qualifications for the position are simply one's ability to manipulate and influence the voters. This is like licensing a doctor because his wife is beautiful. An interesting alternative to the present form of social management is RANDOM representation. That is through a national lottery, where every citizen is eligible for office. This of course would change the emphasis in our educational processes since we would now have a vested interest in training our citizens to be socially responsible and functional.

The emphasis in education would then shift from a competitive social conforming value system to a co-operative motivated value system. Everyone would then have an equal chance of being "President". The liberal arts, social sciences and civics would then become as important or more so than vocational skills and the hard sciences. Inter-active dynamics and the human potential movement would be a necessity, rather than a simple step-child of an educational system based on social conformity (imprisonment of the student) as well as the now dead industrial revolution (mis-management of territory and resources). It would reflect favorably in our daily and civic social interactions.

For example at election lottery time winners will have "won" the privilege to participate in helping govern and harmonize the society. Of these, another group will be randomly selected through the lottery thus filling all positions until the last three winners would form the federal triumvirate. This will decrease the probability of mis-management on any level during any particular term of office, since the level above would be immediately answerable to the level below. The elimination of tenure would reduce the possibility of malfeasance, bribery, and the formation of special interest groups, since no-one would know from one term to the next who would be in power. The harshest punishments of society would be reserved for any government official convicted of taking bribes or misusing power for personal purposes.

Conclusion

We often marvel at the lack of rhyme or reason in the planning for tomorrow. As Gurdjieff has stated — is there life on earth? Or are we just food for the moon? We do not believe that it matters which is correct. What matters is that we reverse the process of cultural absolutism, which holds us prisoners of yesterday and therefore tomorrow. We believe that it is time to view our biology as our destiny, and not the happenstantial regurgitations of housewives and laboring husbands, blindly slaving to produce their replacement cogs in the machine. We believe it is time that we begin to act like the gods we were created to be. "Know ye not that ye are Gods."

We hope we have let no-one off the hook and that everyone will find both something to love and something to hate. Hence this Law is for All!

Finally, if someone asks you how come you are reading such trash, simply tell them that this book is about the nervous system — and when did that become trash? Nor, do not be fooled by the suggestions made in this book, they will not solve your problems, just replace the present ones with something new and hopefully more advanced. If someone asks you for a second time why an intelligent person such as you, is reading such un-evolved junk, just tell them that you are studying for your finals in spiritual-biology. That will assure them that you and the authors are both to be taken seriously.

Lastly, we wish to thank all of the readers who wrote us telling us what a great concept the original edition of this book was. We at Falcon agree, and for some who have asked for an apology, may I quote my dearest friend, now departed, Dr. Israel Regardie "NO!!!! NO!!! NO!!!! A THOUSAND TIMES NO!!!!!"

CHAPTER ONE

IF YOU WANT TO BE SOMEONE
GET OUT OF BED

This book is for each person who wants to get more out of life. However, it is NOT a conventional self-improvement device. It is different from any book you have read because it is designed for those who are willing to work hard for the promised results. If you expect this book to improve your life, make you more happy and free you from unwanted circumstances and experiences you must be willing to change yourself deeply and undo all the non-joyous experiences of the past. Therefore the purpose of this book is help you to experience total JOY and FREEDOM.

**THIS BOOK IS DESIGNED FOR THOSE
WHO ARE TIRED OF BEING
LESS THAN —
WHAT
THEY
COULD
BE**

The way which you will accomplish this is by studying and practicing the techniques, analyzing and synthesizing the images and pictures, and by attempting to understand the deeper message of this book which is revealed by the way it was written and designed.

**IT WILL SHOW YOU THAT YOU ARE BOTH THE JAIL
- THE PRISONER —
AND THE GUARD**

Unlike most books this one will CHALLENGE you, humor you, scare you, insult you, and LOVE you. It is a LIVING -- SPONTANEOUS book and after all that's what life is all about.

I have written about many things, including three specific techniques of ENERGIZED MEDITATION. The EM method is deliberately designed to shake you up. It's designed to get you to change yourself, to *lose* yourself—to rid yourself—to transform yourself into a STAR.

If you have any difficulty with any of the techniques please drop me a short note (I hate to read long letters), and I'll answer your questions.

C☐A☐U☐T☐I☐O☐N

**— THIS AUTHOR PLAYS TRICKS —
SWITCHES SETS — CHANGES STYLE.
STAY ALERT
— READ FURTHER AT YOUR OWN RISK . . . . .**

THE LAB

A lab is a place
where
scientists gather
to test out
their favorite theories.
The reason
they have a lab
is
they realize
they have
more
theories
than
facts.

Unlike most of us who know everything, (If you don't think so just ask anyone about anything and see what happens!—) the real scientist knows that *You* are the Lab, the Subject, and the Experimenter.

Through the process of *ENERGIZED MEDITATION* and other techniques you will "UnDo" all the unwanted experiences of the past which prevent you from living up to your highest potential.

As your own scientist it is important to leave all your preconceived ideas, thoughts and beliefs at the portal of your LAB. This includes your fears, anxieties, uncertainties, doubts and prejudices which have prevented you from experiencing the joy and freedom of your highest aspirations.

WAS

GURDJIEFF

A MONKEY TRAINER?

Gurdjieff, one of the most powerful "real" teachers of "real" self-change, said *LIFE IS REAL ONLY THEN, WHEN "I AM."* His point is clear; we live in a dream — more often a nightmare — which most of the time we are unaware of. Gurdjieff believed that humans are basically robots and have the potential for developing a SOUL and FREE WILL through "work."

Bennett, a student of Gurdjieff, asks a profound question with multiple implications:

"IS

THERE

LIFE

ON

EARTH

?"

The essence of his question is -- what we call human is only potentially human and what we call Life is only the potential for life. Bennett holds that we are machines, stuck in a rut, having difficulty reacting newly and openly to changing situations.

HOW MANY COPIES
WILL THIS BOOK SELL?
THE ONE CLOSEST TO THE EXACT NUMBER
SPENDS A WEEKEND WITH
THE AUTHOR

Some think that to sell books one must be kind and let the reader off the hook. This in my mind is an insult, for the reader deserves to stay on the hook, if he hopes to do more than masturbate. However,

if you wish to masturbate,
I have included some very tantalizing pictures.

The last comment and picture was designed to break your set, your predetermined way of responding to experiences. What effect did it have on you? I was taught this method by a Shinto-Buddhist Monk who, when I approached him with what I thought was a serious (life or death type) question, laughed in my face. Since I was faking enlightenment at that time I just smiled. (Smiling was the thing to do in the 60's particularly if you didn't understand what another person was talking about.)

The point is laughter while being medicinal, also leads to enlightenment. While others ignore earthquakes, atomic bombs, and economic collapse you will be paying full attention but most important - you will be able to laugh.

When

you enter the LAB, laughter will ease your journey.

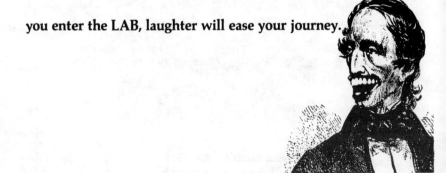

The picture below represents what laughter might do for some of our world leaders, particularly those who lead men to war. Their image portrays again what Bennett meant when he asked his famous question.

Is there Life on Earth?

Conversely,

life in the LAB is quite different. Here everyone is joyous and free. Here man loves life and each act is intended to create joy and freedom rather than misery and restriction.

WHERE DO IDEAS COME FROM?

Many of the ideas in this book come from obscure or unique sources, one of which is a man known as Master Therion. He was a good magician, that is he spent his life trying to UnDo his conditioned self. In the process of this he often offended the sanctimonious section of our society. For this he was labeled a villain. Many including Tim Leary and Bob Anton Wilson credit him as a major influence of the higher consciousness movement of the sixties. Some of my friends and associates felt that by including him in this work, sales and my reputation would be hurt. If this occurs I will be displeased, but my decision to give him his just deserves still stands and to this end I include a picture of Master Therion. For those of you who do not recognize him his identity will be revealed at the proper time.

For those that don't know but would like to guess a few clues are provided.

(1) He enjoyed playing in the Garden of Eros.
(2) He was a poet.
(3) He loved to climb mountains.
(4) He was a mage.
(5) His mother called him a beast.
(6) He wrote a series of books named the Equinox.
(7) He was married more than once and had a number of children.
(8) He was born in the British Empire.
(9) He was a member of the Golden Dawn.

IF YOU WANT
TO **IMPROVE** YOURSELF
GET **RID** OF
YOURSELF
FIRST

Do not misunderstand what I mean by self-improvement. It is not just improving your social personality or mask, nor is it the gathering of information. It first and foremost means "destroying" all that inhibits you from being your true self. Also do not delude yourself that this process is painless for it is not. My definition of self-improvement means "getting rid of what you now call yourself".

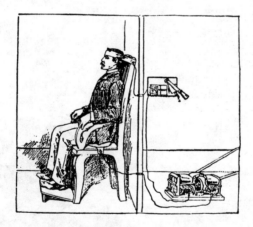

I have written this book with the intention of changing the pre-determined way you have at looking at the world. Often this will require a perspective which you can temporarily use to alter your point of view.

The following theory of "mine" is designed to help you look at the world from a different angle. — — — The process I will discuss is experienced consciously by many people who --- undergo the formula of ——— ———— --- ——— --- —-— UNDOING --- --- —-— themselves. I have labeled it ——THE UNIVERSAL CYCLE OF JOY——. It is derived from Reich's idea of ———————— tension-charge-discharge and relaxation. To understand this idea better view the world and everything in it as a pulsating living organism in constant flux.

Each living thing goes through a cycle of — tension — charge —discharge and relaxation. Everything that is capable of completing this cycle can be labeled as a success. If it can't complete the cycle it can be labeled as a failure and will die without experiencing much joy or happiness. This formula holds true for ants, birds, flowers, people . . .

blue haired old ladies . . .

book buyers, governments . . .

schools . . .

authors . . .

etc. . . .

Each person we know can be categorized as one of four types. A tension type who never builds up a charge.

A charge type who never discharges.

A discharge type who never relaxes.

Well you say that's only three, what about the fourth? That lucky person experiences the joy of going through the whole cycle.

There are many more types in this system, but the more I write about this theory the more I recognize its similarity to other systems. Since it's not original how should the author regard it? More importantly what effect does "originality" have on readers who are more concerned with historical precedents than with the effect information has on their conscious attitude?

This theory will help you define your own particular way of coping with life. Make a list of your activities and then analyze each of them in terms of where you stop on the cycle of tension—charge—discharge and relaxation. Look at the way you eat, talk, love, walk, think, feel, and etc.

Is this author really concerned about the originality of this theory or is he simply communicating the pettiness and "academic stupidity" that is so rampant in the field of "higher consciousness"?

If you choose to expand this "used" but novel approach, take into consideration interaction effects. Look at the strengths and weaknesses of various phases. Consider the effects of age, sex, health, genetics, environmental influences, and child rearing practices.

Now that I have given you an example of a theory, the next idea is to turn that into an experiment. Put the theory to work, try it out. How valid is it? Where do your leaders fit? Where do I fit? Where do you fit?

This section of Chapter One presents some very ancient ideas that have been gleaned from various sources including the Golden Dawn, Tantra Yoga, and Zen. The ideas and concepts are very real and require some study to achieve their desired effects. These are advanced techniques and are presented here in case some of you feel adventurous and would like to get into something which will blow your mind right now.

The only way out is in. If you want out of your theories and your jails, start by being a COSMIC SCIENTIST. When you do that long enough you will become a COSMIC COMIC. The theory of open-end-ed-ness requires that you first become UN-DONE;

THE COSMIC COMIC

then and only then can you start advanced LAB work. If you believe that there is more to life than the mundane program which has been prepared for you — — — you are on the right track.

Freedom comes from the knowledge of the *Orphic Mysteries*. Life oscillates between chaos and form. Try on a form, use it —know it—discard it.

Then from chaos make a new form. Repeat the Cycles as often as possible and you will feel alive and free.

CHAOS IS ALWAYS PRESENT

— AND IT —

COMES IN VARIOUS SHAPES AND SIZES

Buy a copy of Wilson's — that is Bob Anton — *Cosmic Trigger*. **Read it once. Now buy a copy of his** *Prometheus Rising*.

Now read that. Place it aside. Now pick up a copy of Israel Regardie's secret tape, — — *The Grinning Giggling Monkey Faced Guru and the Pig song*. **Listen to that three times.**

Time to read again. S.M.I.^{2}L.E. through a copy of Tim Leary's *Info-Psychology*. **Now read this book again, and then re-read the** *COSMIC TRIGGER* **while you play Dr. Regardie's tape. After you have completed this, turn on Dr. Regardie's** *Mantram Tape*. **Listen to the Mantram tape for 6-8 hours.**

Now re-read this book. When you have reached this point, rest for two days, or longer, when you finish resting, re-read the *Cosmic Trigger*, while playing the *MANTRAM TAPE*. Now stand on your head and re-read *Info-Psychology*. If you can do all this, you will start to get the idea of what I mean by the Cosmic Scientist and the Cosmic Comic.

If you decide to do this experiment, I suggest that you do it exactly as I described it. We have and it works best that way. You can order everything you need from the PUBLISHER who bravely put this book in print.

SEX AND CHAOS

The following SECTION was written after the Author invented a game called Chaotic Sex. There is nothing magical or secret about Chaotic Sex, except that it requires a knowledge of the Hebrew alphabet. Once you have memorized the 22 letters, which correspond to certain paths on the Tree of Life, find yourself a willing partner, and proceed to teach him or her the alphabet by taking on the various positions of the letters. If you have the perseverance and the fortitude to make it through the entire series you will have UNDONE yourself and will never feel boredom in the area of sex again.

A TRIBUTE TO ——

I have heard a rumor recently that Tim Leary is really Abe (Ape) Lincoln. While I don't know what Tim thinks of this association I wish to explore the possibility.

TIMOTHY
LEARY

The story goes that Abe freed the slaves from their imprisonment, torture and humiliation. In the same way Tim Leary has shown us that we too are slaves to our instincts, imprinting and learning. Until --- we wake up ——— we are primate slaves. We live in a tunnel reality which is pri-mately concerned with the desire to consume and the fear of being consumed. This occurs literally in more "primitive" cultures and metaphorically at the ego level in more "advanced" cultures. We literally accept how and what we "are" and dare not question the meaning, origin and purpose of our fundamental personality traits, values and behavior.

We elect and look up to authorities who are no more than "smart" monkeys who know how to play on our primate fears. Some of us even feel gratitude to our guards, and many of us are even willing to die for them.

We accept our imprisonment as a necessary requirement for "order" and survival.

Tim Leary has shown us a way out! He has shown us that we can change our own brains according to "our" own will. He has shown us that "we can remake our picture of ourselves and the universe we live in."

Our sleeping Brain is capable of anything and everything we wish. The solution to man's "problems" lies in first getting "himself" out of his own way, and then re-programming his brain according to his "true will". Man's freedom is not in his conditioned ego-personality or his castrated visions of gods and demons but in his desire and ability to change himself.

Tim is the Abe (Ape) Lincoln not of just a race, but of the "Human" Race, and to this end we give our vote to him, not as President, for that is a low circuit job, but as a NEURO-LOGIC—ADVENTURER. I hope this little explanation will put the rumor to rest.

N☐O☐T☐I☐C☐E

Falcon Press feels so strongly about the Great Liberator, Dr. Timothy Leary, that we have joined with Tim to produce a revision of his brilliant Future History series written during the time of the Great Persecution.

As you read this notice did you have an instantaneous, negative reaction to Dr. Leary's name? If so, it is now time for you to turn to Chapter Four of this book. Then get a copy of *Info-Psychology*, a revision of *Exo-Psychology*, read it through once and then re-read Chapter Four.

CHAPTER TWO

TO KNOW ENLIGHTENMENT
NOT TO JUST KNOW OF IT
A ZEN STATEMENT

You must give up the thing most precious to you.
            You must give up the thing which you love so dearly,
the thing that you hold on to
- you must give it up -
- you must give it up. -

There can be no half-way measures in "finding"
            ENLIGHTENMENT.
It is not hiding anywhere.
It is HERE and NOW.

You must see that you are frightened,
that something is at STAKE all the time —
even in your dreams — something is at stake,
ALL THE TIME.

Everything which shocks you,
disrupts you, disturbs you can be your friend.
Everything which allows you to sleep,
to be complacent
hinders you.

To become in Accordance with your
            TRUE POTENTIAL,
you must be in Discordance with yourself.

YOU ARE AT STAKE ALL THE TIME
AND YOU LOOK FOR FOOD WHICH FEEDS YOU

Anything which delays your end ——
    feeds you.
You digest this diet overabundant with FAT.
You are insatiable,
and require constant FAT to keep you going.
You use more energy and power maintaining
    THE ILLUSION
of your insatiable dream than Living.
You will even STRUT to death's window.

    But to Know the DEATHLESS ONE —
you — the **strutter — must die.**
You must go on a diet — then
Starve to DEATH.

You must stop finding yourself in misery,
in cranial pride,
— and historic stupidity.

    You must stop strutting around like a
fattened COW.

You must stop bowing down to your mistakes.
You must stop your idol worshipping.
You must surrender your misery.

You must stop acting surprised when
something happens to you

FOR -- it is the same old thing.
You must stop reacting to things
as you always HAVE.
You must stop proving your story.
You must stop extending the past
into the present and future.

You must stop defending your stupidity,
-- YOUR SLEEP.
You must stop defending
YOUR MISERY.

YOU MUST WAKE UP

You even forsake your health to feed this Monster.
He drinks your blood,
this friend of yours.
You will sacrifice anything and everything to feed him.

Everyone and everything is food for you.
How people treat you (good-bad) is food for you.
You are so weak yet He is so strong.
Why do you prefer the insatiable one to HIM?

You oppose — you conform — all is food for you.
You agree — you disagree — all is food for you.
You render opinions on this and that,
and spout authorities to back you up
— all is food for you.
You are surrounded by friends or alone —
all is food for you.
You are naked or adorned —
all is food for you.

SOMETHING IS **ALWAYS**
AT STAKE
SOMETHING IS ALWAYS ON THE LINE.

You strut around
proud of the misery
you have caused yourself.
You will do anything to preserve the misery.
You will fight,
you will sneer,
you will accuse,
you will blame,   nothing can satiate
you will steal,   millions can not
you will hide,   fame can not
— all to preserve fear!   love can not
REMEMBER   power can not
THERE IS ALWAYS   friends can not
SOMETHING   ONLY HIM.
AT STAKE.
THAT SOMETHING IS YOU.

AFTER YOU HAVE IT ALL THEN WHAT?

victories feed you
your failures feed you
Your past feeds you
your ideas feed you

if your friends allow you to be complacent,
accept or like you that is food for you.
If they hate you, that is food for you.

WHY ARE YOU SO HUNGRY?

Does death not even inspire your appetite?
Do you know death?
Or do you just have snapshots of it?
You act like you are immune from it,
that it just happens all around you
-- but not to you.
Not even your own death can shudder you
move you from your -- feeding frenzy.

WHAT FOOD IS NEXT?

Misery is food,
and you can find plenty of that.
You are never at a loss for that.

You never learn
because MISERY is food
You repeat the same mistake,
the same mistake,
the same misery
over and over.

Worst of all
you do it with *pride*.
with your sneer of superiority,
WITH A SENSE OF NEWNESS,
with a sense of uniqueness,
with a sense of choice,
or with a sense of helplessness.

Yet, it is the same mistake,
the same misery.

You do not even dare find a NEW MISTAKE
              A NEW MISERY

since that might wake you up from your
              FEEDING FRENZY

(Zen carries many kinds of sticks. For one cloaked in laughter read
Camden Benares' *Zen Without Zen Masters*.)

TECHNIQUE

When you speak to others notice your Dead phrases, and your
patterned stylized responses. They are indications that you are
sound asleep. You have something at stake each time you repeat
these habitual phrases and comments.

Find your patterned-machine like phrases which you use over and
over again and hold so dearly. Count the number of times you use
them in a three day period, and then:

STOP

STOP

STOP

STOP

Stay Awake
and each time you prepare to repeat
this DEAD TONE -----

STOP

Say Stop to yourself.
Each time this stammered crippled phrase
rears its Frightened head

STOP

BE SILENT.

Then if you truly know who and what you are,

SAY IT SILENTLY

WAKE — — UP

EVERY MAN AND EVERY WOMAN IS A STAR

CHAPTER THREE

THE EXPERIMENTER
Do not lust after results
Frater P.

The experimenter by definition must be more clear than the subject.

A requirement to perform your own work is the ability to look at yourself as you are — not as you wish to be. By the way many of the "wish to be's" are simply bullshit, and belong to the subject and not to the experimenter. I don't want to hear any crap about how you just want to help people, or how you just want to be happy. If you want to do these things you first must BE YOURSELF, and that means undoing yourself.

Refer to the previous section if you are becoming confused. If after undoing yourself you still have the same "wish to be's" then you can believe they are more valid.

As an experimenter with your own LAB and subject(s) you are obligated to view things as clearly and tentatively as possible. Don't start believing in FINALISMS, until you have enough experience doing the WORK. There are levels of ability as an experimenter, and your results will become more valid as you progress up the scale.

Do not get pre-occupied with grades however, (For Information On This Folly read Israel Regardie's book *My Rosicrucian Adventure*, republished in 1982 by FALCON PRESS Under the title *What You Should Know About the Golden Dawn*) to get a feel for those who are more pre-occupied with GRADES than RESULTS.

As an experimenter it is important to realize that disappointment is a necessary result of THE GREAT WORK. Life and experience operate in cycles. Become aware that all things go through cycles.

ONE way of looking at the cycles of life is as follows:

1. First there is inspiration and enthusiasm.
2. Next there is frustration and disappointment, laziness, despair, and fear of failure. This is where most people give up, get depressed and regress into fantasy.
3. Re-newed Effort and Enthusiasm.
4. RESULTS—-satisfaction. NOTE: I said satisfaction-results, not success or failure. Being the most Honest Man In The World, I did not give you a "WISH TO BE." I don't know for sure what your results will be, and you don't either.

You must be willing to complete the CYCLE. If you do, the

freedom and joy which is your rightful heritage will find a permanent home in your heart.

YOU ARE AN OPEN ENDED SYSTEM

Even when this UNIVERSE disappears experimentation will never cease. The fluctuating process of expansion and contraction will remain as the primary creative element of Becoming.

FEAR

Fear is failure. I will repeat this from time to time. You will experience fear in the LAB, but do not succumb to it, just breathe your way through it, or if necessary scream your way through it.

Most values, beliefs, opinions and behavior are the result of deep, preconscious fear and survival tension. When we are not aware of the power that these primal feelings have over our lives, we develop secondary feelings of hate, greed and envy. As these are interpersonally

unacceptable, we balance these powerful feelings with guilt, [another word for fear turned to self-hate] internal deadness, blame, hostility, depression, superiority, and inferiority. These defenses are inadequate, outworn and destructive methods of coping with the primary animal instinct for survival. **Man, to** *Become more than Human,* **must fully recognize the power of these feelings before he can take appropriate measures to outgrow their influence.** However, most humans tend to ignore their true motivations and instead re-label their fear and survival anxieties as duty, business, concern, love, help, protection, security, morality, obligation, patriotism, need, opinion, etc. The result of this personal and inter-personal deceit is stagnation and turmoil.

DO NOT BELIEVE ANY SYSTEM WHICH TELLS YOU IT HAS THE ANSWER.
IT IS STERILE, DEAD AND
DANGEROUS

Answers such as those promised On How To Achieve Enlightenment While Still Being Our Good Old Neurotic Selves, are fractional, stifling, degrading and outright stupid.

The battle for your own LAB will be never ending. Possessing your own LAB is not consistent with any Power system, since the LAB produces no currency which it can de-value. You will not find a course in LAB work in any structured system, since each LAB is a STAR.

The techniques and methods presented will help you protect what is yours, once you have found it. There are more methods but these are best done under supervision of someone who has a LAB and knows the score ....

HOW TO BUILD YOUR OWN LAB
AND BE YOUR OWN EXPERIMENTER

Pictures and symbols have as much to say as words, sometimes even more and on occasion they mean nothing ("Yeh! Sure, I don't believe a word he says -- that lying Robot.")

This book should give you the necessary clues to rid yourself of enough conditioned neurons so that you can give yourself the grade of Zelator, in THIS SYSTEM. It does not give you the grade of Zelator in OTHER SYSTEMS, but between you and me if you did your work with sincerity, you're probably better than a Zelator in other systems—but this is just between you and me. I can imagine the flack I'd get if this were made public.

Be conscious at all times of your uniqueness, that your LAB has something to contribute if you do your experiments.

All experiments are valid, no matter if your results contradict those of another experimenter. The only thing which invalidates any experiment is contamination caused by self-deceit.

This, I hope, will not happen. If it does happen re--examine your method, re--examine yourself — purge yourself of further conditioned neurons, no matter what the consequences.

PURGE — PURGE — PURGE

THE ORAL * * * * * * * * * * ANAL * * * * * PIT

Throughout the process of Living -- the oral — anal pit will pose the most danger. Experiments are most frequently sabotaged by the — — give me — give me — I'm about to die -- or -- this is mine and shortly I'll have yours. The oral-anal pit can be referred to as 333. If you don't know what that number means please look it up.

Images — forces — powers from the pit will jump up at any time attempting to scare and intimidate you. To control this I suggest starting your most serious experiments with the appropriate banishing ritual or with a working knowledge of motivational and learning theory, together with some information on statistical — — — theory. (The Banishing Ritual sounds a lot simpler.)

If you don't know a banishing ritual use the one from *The Complete Golden Dawn System of Magic* by Israel Regardie. A tape demonstrating this Ritual has been recorded by Regardie and can be ordered from Falcon Press. (While I may or may not be the most Honest man in the World I do belive in selling good material, hence the constant reference to the materials offered by Falcon Press.)

Also I get a commission or something like that — — — I think.

... and now a word from our sponsors

IS **FALCON PRESS*** A TOOL OF THE *ILLUMINATI CONSPIRACY?*

Which Are You?

FUTANTS LOVE US — FOSSILS HATE US

* If we aren't in trouble we ain't doin' our job!

STATEMENT OF PURPOSE

Falcon Press is dedicated to bringing intelligence and immortality to the Planet Earth. Why are *YOU* here?

Do what thou wilt shall be the whole of the Law.

Love is the law, love under will.

TO CLEAR THE MIND
OF ITS NOISE
THEN TO LOSE THE MIND ALTOGETHER

THIS IS MEDITATION

OF COURSE SOME WOULD CALL THIS INSANITY

To achieve Enlightenment (The Real Knowledge That You Are A Robot And Have Been Programmed, And That You Can Re-Program Your Brain According To Your True Will.) you must first put yourself aside.

The Wisdom and Freedom of the Great Work (becoming more than human) is available to everyone who is willing to work and give up the security and stupidity of collective humanity.

YOU ARE SEEKING

A

NEW

YOU

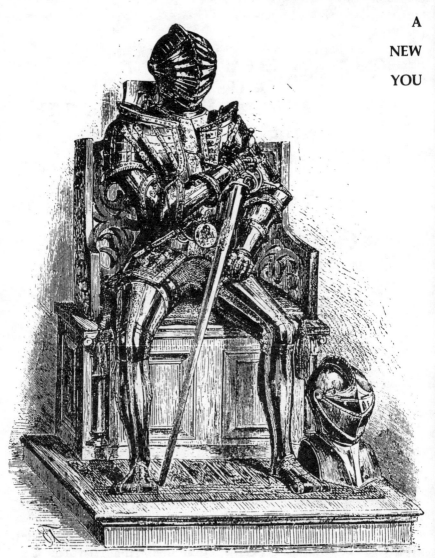

The new you or higher you resides in the ability to re-program your own brain according to your own will.

— The "you" which you are familiar with has been created through years of random, blind and unconscious programming. It is the result of happenstance, genetics and history. It has as much relationship to your Real Self, as freedom to fascism.

(Much to the shock of those in power, what we are is relative programmers -- that is our brain is a neural garden of growing fibers and chemicals which in the final analysis we can learn to program ourselves, but first we must do away with the roots and fertilizers which do not fit our True Nature and Will.)

Now the time has come when everyone on the planet must take the responsibility for Self-Re-Programming. Matter is perfecting itself and we will find that it is centered in our consciousness. Therefore, to be prepared for the coming Universal Expansion our machined selves must be outfitted with new neural patterns.

Never lose the awareness that you have the ability to re-program your own brain according to your will.

Humans have the outrageous habit of believing that once a pattern is established it must remain. This is particularly true when it concerns our "sacred" personality and characteristics.

YOU HAVE TO GO

AGAIN?

It is difficult for most of humanity to believe that how they feel, what they think, how they act, and what they believe is LEARNED, and there is nothing special or unique about them which is not contributed to by genetics and conditioning. To repeat —— all that we hold sacred about ourselves is not of our own choosing, but rather a result of "chance". However, unlike other animals humans are capable of willing, choosing, creating an identity through the process of self-undoing and then reconstruction.

Yet most of us become insulted, hurt or violent if anyone dare question the worth of the junk and burdens which fill our minds, hearts and attics.

We slaughter entire populations over ideas, values and psycho-territoriality which we did not consciously choose. We have automatically accepted our selves and values without even knowing we have, nor do most have the ability to question the nature and purpose of our thoughts and behavior. We have, like monkeys, blindly imitated the authorities of youth.

Our egos are often so weak and vulnerable that we tend to create conflict over ourselves wherever we go, and whomever we are with. Our sense of pride, possession and territory, propel us into action of which we are often ashamed, for we occasionally realize that we have acted more like a crazed monkey than the real human we have the potential to be. The mass of humanity is so unconscious of this that we tacitly and even worse -- openly -- accept our monkey-like behavior as a necessary standard of life.

The truth is we are constantly being programmed by parents, friends, ads, authors, radios, movies, t.v., teachers and politicians. Finally these programs become so much a part of us, that we begin to question our every thought and action in terms of these programs.

Much of it has been subliminal — so subtle, so continuous, so normal, so common, that you are not aware that some system either blindly or intentionally mis-uses you for their POWER needs; and has

been cleverly persuading you to accept a given system of beliefs and values. So cleverly that your unconscious mind is gobbling up every suggestion, even the suggestion to *question things* — in a prescribed fashion of course:

-— without ever your True Conscious Self suspecting what was going on. And these beliefs which have been programmed into your computer without your awareness are now - YOU — operating in certain predictable fashions to certain stimuli -- again without your being aware of the fact that you are REACTING instead of simply ACTING of your own free will. (Of course I'm not talking about *you*. To learn more about how this works for everyone else read Steven Heller's *Monsters and Magical Sticks — There's No Such Thing as Hypnosis?* especially Chapter IV, "Forget It.")

But now time is running out. If we are to survive—individually or globally, each of us has an awesome responsibility to awaken from our robot-like sleep and become aware of what is going on. Never before in the history of mankind has the human race been capable of destroying itself and yet at the same time having the potential for total freedom and "god-ship".

The cosmic drama is being enacted within all of our lives in varying degrees; without exception everyone of us is being forced to look into the face of disaster — be it economic, emotional, or spiritual.

Disaster, unnecessary pain, death and dementia are probably not necessary particularly if we learn how to perform Magick (which simply means *Brain Change Willed*). Crowley defined magick as ... "the Science and Art of causing Change to occur in conformity with the Will." Eliphas Levi, the great 19th century occultist, believed that in order to reign over ourselves, we first must learn "how" to will. The invoking of these authorities is to help those unfamiliar with the true purpose and nature of magick to realize that there is no mumbo jumbo involved, but a science of self-change.

THESE SNARES AND
NEURONS BELONG TO

....

Many are blind and are unaware of what they face; they look with unseeing eyes and blank faces.

Unfortunately, blindness and blankness of expression will not provide protection. In the days ahead there is no safety except that which can be obtained from Undoing Yourself and then Re-making Yourself.

The body must be free from the Robotic Mind and allowed to express itself freed from all snares. And finally the Mind must become a SLAVE of the True Will.

Only in the service of the Will is there perfect freedom. Man has always been proud of his vaunted Free Will. In reality, Free Will as it is publicly referred to is a fallacy. The average person's concept of free will is license to worship one's conditioned neurons.

The famous Swiss psychologist, Carl Jung, provides a more accurate definition:

> "Freedom of will is the ability to do gladly
> that which I must do."

CHALLENGE ——— BRAIN ——— GOD —·— WILL

In the new age man will be faced with gigantic challenges presented by his ever expanding conscious brain and its extended technology.

In the end the only God a conscious person can admire is the God of Will.

CONSCIOUSNESS AND TENSION

The two factors we have to be most concerned with are Consciousness and Tension. As you become more astute in achieving deep relaxation, you will realize that you can have complete control of your life through the ability to reprogram your mind. However, to accomplish this you must first learn to reduce all un—necessary tension and stress.

It is safe (and most of us do play it that way) to say that the majority of our problems arise from the lack of consciousness of our programming and the belief that we are more or less helpless in changing our condition. The problem we now face is that of becoming conscious of our programming, and developing the willingness to change those things which our robot holds so dear.

Existence itself (up to now) is dependent upon the conflict between two opposing forces. Psychological studies have proven that tension is produced by happy experiences as well as depressing ones. Tension is a fact of life — and not necessarily an unfortunate fact either. Stresses and strains are not only an integral part of life, but they often appear as life itself. But to bring about the change in consciousness necessary to achieve self programming, we must use some powerful techniques to reduce tension. A still mind is needed for re-programming. This is a result of Meditation, though this may not have been the intent of the meditator. Keep in mind your goal, together with the reasons for it: to free the body from the snares of the Mind, and to make the Mind a Slave to the Unconditioned Will.

Meditation is as old as time itself, but the needs of each new generation differ from those of the -- preceding one -- requiring a re-definition of purpose and the re-formulation of technique.

Energized Meditation is such an adaptation developed by combining Eastern and Western information. Over 20 years have been spent in practice and research to develop a method which would benefit those who seek the goal of "Brain Change Willed."

EM is a sensory-tonic (muscular) technique which takes into account the fact that tension is thought, and thought is tension. Every thought has its neuro-sensate-muscular equivalent. Conversely every tension can be converted into a thought. Every twitch and sensation conveys a thought or a meaning.

A STILL MIND
IS NECESSARY?

It has been suggested from the beginning of meditative practices that the Mind is the final obstacle to Enlightenment. (*This is not to imply that the Mind is Evil, or some sort of destructive force. It does imply however that the Mind once set on a program is self-propelling and difficult to alter. For further information see* **Prometheus Rising** *by Robert Anton Wilson, particularly the section which discusses the idea of "What the Thinker Thinks -- The Prover Proves".*) The mind's major by-product, thought, must be harnessed so that in the end "Mind" itself can be reee--programmed, not just of content but of the "way" it operates as well. It follows that to destroy all unnecessary tension frees the Mind from its programmed thoughts. This in turn will make the task of EGO-MIND re-programming (transcendence) easier. In order to clear the mind of thought, each sensate-muscle group must be cleared of tension, or at least the tension must be reduced. The technical aspects of this idea are overwhelming. While meditation reduces tension, tension also reduces the result of meditation. For this reason concentration on a mantra can never be achieved to complete satisfaction. This is one of the major problems to which Energized Meditation addresses itself. Mantra focus is necessary in the beginning and intermediate stages of meditation, but in order to actually become the Mindless One, the Deathless One, all tension-thought-image structures must finally disappear. True merging with the Universal Programmer (Leary's Higher Circuits) only occurs when Your lower circuits are "clear" and lack domination. What most of us call I — You — Ego are sets and webs of interactive and interwoven tensions. While to some extent these are presently necessary for functioning in this social world, they have become the rival of true conscious will.

THE DESTRUCTION
OF THOUGHT AND TENSION

Energized Meditation destroys tension and thought, allowing the student of the LAB to experience complete mindlessness, and Union with Consciousness. This ·state is an excellent beginning for re-programming the mind.

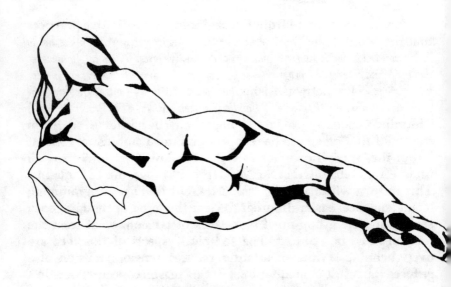

Not wishing to stimulate more thought-tension we will not at this time try to compare or contrast this method with others. We will get down to facts which in the end can only be verified for you -- by you -- in your own LAB. Do not believe or accept this theory or in fact any other theory and this does include all theories which have previously been accepted as true, without complete testing and proof. But remember Wilson,

"What the Thinker Thinks -- The Prover Proves."

MENTAL CHATTER
AND
SUB—VOCAL
TRANSMISSIONS

Before we get into the first segment of this technique let me make you aware of some facts. Constant mental chattering or thought creates tensions. When you are thinking your voice box moves ever so slightly as thoughts are flowing through your mind. In addition, the jaw moves slightly, as well as the tongue and the eyes. In fact, as stated before there is a fine state of tension when we are thinking. So to achieve true Mindlessness, we first must become aware of the facial, throat, and neck tension which are associated with thinking.

EXPERIMENT I

Sit or lie down in a quite place and allow yourself to "think" about anything. Notice how and where your thinking is experienced. Notice what motions and tensions exist in your face-neck-throat area. After you have completed this, "think" about something unpleasant and notice if there is any difference. Now try "thinking" about something pleasant and make the same notations. Once you are thoroughly aware of this, attempt the following:

EXPERIMENT II

Lie down and do not move. Just breathe normally with your eyes closed. Now become aware and describe out loud for 15 minutes every sensation and muscle twitch in your body. Become aware that tension exists all around and within you.

These two experiments should be tried three times over a week to help you verify that tension is thought — thought is tension. This will require 45 minutes — 15 minutes for each trial. If you do not experience the voice box -- facial sensation, or if you are not aware of anything during experiment II, double the time.

METHOD I

Step 1. Sit or lie down. Make Faces -- Stretch all the muscles in the face. Open your mouth as wide as you can, move the jaw from side to side. At the same time open your eyes as wide as you can. Move your eyes up and down and from side to side. This will begin to destroy tension, thereby destroying uncontrolled and extraneous thoughts generated by this area. Make many different faces. Do this for about 2-3 minutes. (*A word of caution: While in the end these exercizes are meant to reduce and eliminate certain thought patterns, some might find an increase of new thoughts from previously "Hidden" places of the mind. If this is the case don't be concerned, since this will be a fine way to perform "mental house cleaning."*)

Step II. Hum and Chatter -- Hum from the depths of your voice box. Use OM or just MMMM. Do this for 1-2 minutes. Now using your tongue, chatter — DA DA — BA BA BA. Stick out your jaw as far as you can and continue humming and chattering. Do this for 2-3 minutes.

Step III. Shoulders to Ears -- Pull your shoulders up as if you were trying to reach your ears. When they start feeling tired, drop them as low as you can. Repeat this 3 times in 2-3 minute intervals.

Step IV. Nose Breathing -- With your mouth closed take in a deep breath inflating your chest and pulling your stomach up. Be sure to pull the belly in. Hold for a 7 count and then just let the chest fall and the belly relax. Repeat this 10-20 times. Be sure to allow an additional 7 count to elapse before your next inhalation.

Step V. Turn Head -- Now bring your attention to your head and turn it from side to side as far as you can. Repeat for 2-3 minutes.

Step VI. Leg Stretch -- Lying down on your back, hold your legs about 4 inches off the ground and stretch outward. Hold this as long as you can then let them drop. Repeat this 2-3 times.

Step VII. Quick Breath -- With your mouth slightly open breathe rapidly, sighing as you exhale. Do this for 2-3 minutes.

Now lie down and sense and feel your body, for about 10 --— minutes. Note every sensation you feel. Now assume a meditative position of your choice making sure that:

(1) Your eye lids are not tightly closed, but simply relaxed.

(2) That your jaw is relaxed and not tense. Make sure of this by trying to stick out your tongue; if you have to lower your jaw, it was too tightly held. Check your forehead making sure it is not wrinkled. Once you are relaxed, either concentrate on your mantra or point of focus. For those students who do not have a mantra or point, we suggest Dr. Regardie's Mantram tape or simply OOOOO-OOOMMMMMMM. For students who wish or require specific images or points of focus, please feel free to contact us.

(3) Finally make sure your throat is not blocked by holding your head in the wrong position. Make sure it is straight. In order to reduce thoughts, keep the eyes relaxed and still, with your tongue touching the roof of your mouth. Do not move the larynx and again be sure that your jaw is relaxed. Meditate before eating, or wait for 2-3 hours after eating a heavy meal. It is also best if the bladder and bowels have been emptied before you start your work.

HOW MANY TIMES A DAY DO YOU BREAK THE LAW?

Do what thou wilt shall be the whole of the Law.
      -- I am leaving out an important line -- What is it?
Man has the right to live by his own law.
Man has the right to live in the way that he wills to do.
Man has the right to dress as he wills to do.
Man has the right to dwell where he wills to dwell.
Man has the right to move as he will on the face of the Earth.

Man has the right to eat what he will.
Man has the right to drink what he will.
Man has the right to think what he will.
Man has the right to speak as he will.
Man has the right to write as he will.
Man has the right to mould as he will.
Man has the right to carve as he will.
Man has the right to work as he will.
Man has the right to rest as he will.
Man has the right to love as he will, where, when and with whom
         he will.
Man has the right to die when and how he will.
Man has the right to kill those who would thwart these rights.

By: Master Therion

Master Therion is a freer of slaves. It is very easy to understand why he is hated by Dogma addicts and pushers.

These laws represent enlightened anarchy! This means living without dictators, if you can imagine that. Dictators know that "humans" prefer anything which looks like ORDER, no matter how stifling, rather than anything which looks like freedom. The solution --- tell them they are free ——— show them that they are --- slaves.

For further information read the *Masks Of The Illuminati, The Tao Teh King,* and *The Eye In The Triangle.*

CHAPTER FOUR

DOGMA JUNKIES

Dogma is a drug -- and you are a dogma addict.

"But Doctor, what is Dogma?" "Well, dogma is acting as though you possess absolute truth. Some words which are similar are -- dictatorial, stubborn, egotistical, bigoted, fanatical, intolerant, opinionated, overbearing, arrogant, stupid, despotic, and the list continues."

DOGMA MIS—CONCEPTIONS

From the day you were born you have been fed dogma by *your dogma junkies.* Now you are a dogma addict -- addicted just like a heroin addict except, unlike heroin *your addiction is so common that it goes unnoticed.*

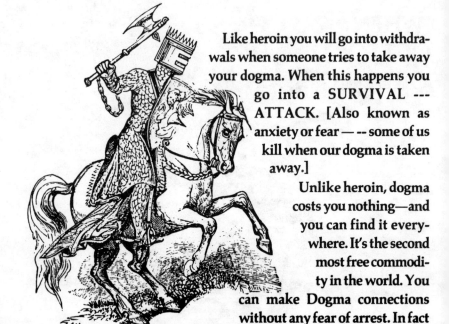

Like heroin you will go into withdrawals when someone tries to take away your dogma. When this happens you go into a SURVIVAL --- ATTACK. [Also known as anxiety or fear — -- some of us kill when our dogma is taken away.]

Unlike heroin, dogma costs you nothing—and you can find it everywhere. It's the second most free commodity in the world. You can make Dogma connections without any fear of arrest. In fact you are rewarded for spreading the junk. Dogma is the *LSD* of the -- (Status Quo) -- and like LSD -- dogma creates hallucinations which we commonly share.

The process of dogmatization is so important that institutions have been erected for the protection and dissemination of the Drug.

WHEN YOU GO OUT FOR DINNER ORDER DOGMA

"ITS CHEAP"

If someone spots you going into dogma withdrawal (finding or following your Own True Will) you will be provided with a remedy -- be it sympathy, electro-shock therapy or, as in Dr. Leary's case, --incarceration.

Dogma (it is interesting for those of us who have learned to spell backwords that dogma is **AmGod**) is essential for the maintenance and protection of those in power.

DOGMA SPEED

The junk travels faster than the speed of light. If the speed of dogma transmission becomes slower than the speed of change then a nervous breakdown can occur. When this happens frantic attempts are made to find fresh dogma to fill the gap. Our social system is full of fresh connections, ranging from psychiatrists, who are specialists in dogma breakdown and withdrawal, T.V., affairs, shopping sprees, wars, sickness, economic disaster, chaos, counter cultures, laws, moralities, etc.

CREATING DOGMA DEMAND AND TRADE INS

Survival attacks can be programmed into your system by the Status Quo DEALERS. Dealers motivate, foster and create survival attacks so they can feed you relief. They gently return you back to your equilibrated state of DOGMA HIGH. This gives them a credit in your DOGMA BANK (guilt, fear and "responsibility"), which they can later call in -- particularly if they need you to do something which would be against your better judgment (such as getting killed in a DOGMA BATTLE (wars, riots, etc.).

INTELLIGENT DOGMA

The most advanced DOGMA JUNKIES are of course the educated addicts. They "CHOOSE" their -- DOGMA -- carefully, not knowing of course that they're junkies. They evaluate themselves and others in terms of the logic-reason-justice of their DOGMA and -- the customary paraphernalia (styles, conventions, common sense, good taste and consensus).

PUSHERS
AND
DEALERS

Dogma pushers and dealers come in various sizes and shapes, but at least 25% of the culture is in the direct business of pushing DOGMA free of charge. The remaining 75% are in the business of creating demand and selling the junk for a decent profit. Dogma pushers are constantly selling, controlling and monopolizing the market. If you shop carefully many of them give rebates. What Dogma have you bought today?

DOGMA ILLNESS

When better theories threaten to take the place of worn out dogma the Old Pushers experience Survival--Attacks. Without much warning they--attack it-- kill it, jail it, ostracize it, or in some cases cure it--another word for Brain-Washing. The last gimmick is a recent

development used most openly in the USSR, and is normally labeled as treatment. Instead of murder or torture, they now treat those who wish to escape from dogma addiction. An ill person is someone who has created a Survival--Attack in (threatened) the wrong person or group. When this happens, the "experts" are called in to provide the necessary treatment to "help" the victim back to health (DOGMA CONSUMPTION). Treatment also helps the patient become part of the FABRIC of Society (also known as useful, aka as predictable, aka as bored, etc.

IN SEARCH FOR NEW CONNECTIONS

In the search for Dogma we find humans frantically running from place to place, person to person, belief to belief, doubt to doubt, pain to pain, euphoria to euphoria. They are doing everything in the world possible to prevent withdrawal and Survival—Attacks. In order for them to understand one another a Dogma language is necessary. I have reproduced a few choice words for your consumption:

**1.
CONSTIPATED
DOGMAMITES**

These consist of those who are collecting junkie checks from the Pushers, for their loyalty to the connection. Also known as employees for the government and/or major corporations.

**2.
DIARRHEA
AM—GOD**

Here we have two groups, a. (Those in charge of marketing and research.) b. (Those about to be voted out of office.)

3.
FOOD FOR DOGMA
Parents and potential parents.
Most people lose what was left of their exploratory drive
when they become parents.
Some say its like having the last nail driven into the coffin.
Of course this doesn't have to happen,
but more often than not it does.

4.
RAW MATERIAL
Infants, Children and Teen-agers.

5. DOGMA BUSTERS.
Leary, Crowley, Wilson,
Regardie, and many more.
See Timothy Leary's
The Intelligence Agents.

6. JUNKIES.
Everyone,
except you
of course.

7. DOGMA PATROLLERS. Those in uniform and out. We are blessed in this country with a multitude of protectors and watchers. Are you one of them? If so drop me a line so I can include your comments in my next book.

8. HEALERS. Those professionals that try to get you to fit in again when you finally start thinking for "yourself".

9. DOGMA SCRIBES. They argue over the rights and wrongs of everything. More often than not they create more problems than they solve. This helps their income, for they are commonly known as lawyers and politicians.

10. AM—GOD. The Teachers
of self-hate. This includes only
those whose vocabulary consists
of words or phrases (75% or more)
of "right, wrong, can't,
thou shall not,
should, etc."

11. DOGMA HEALTH. Dogma by democracy. The magical ability to reduce the highest to the lowest. To quote A.C., "The single argument that can be adduced in favour of an Enlightened Democracy is that it provides more completely for the fooling of the Sovereign People than any other known system."

12. MARRIAGE. The ability to turn love and instinct into A—BORED—DOG. Also a license to stop treating human beings like human beings. A decree which states that you must respect someone elses dirty habits, etc., etc.

13. FREE—LOVE. Sex without the benefit of boredom AND observers.

14. HIGH HOPE. The Latest Dogma.

15. LOW HOPE. Used Dogma.

16. DOGMA DAYS. National holidays where the Robots are allowed more time off without supervision

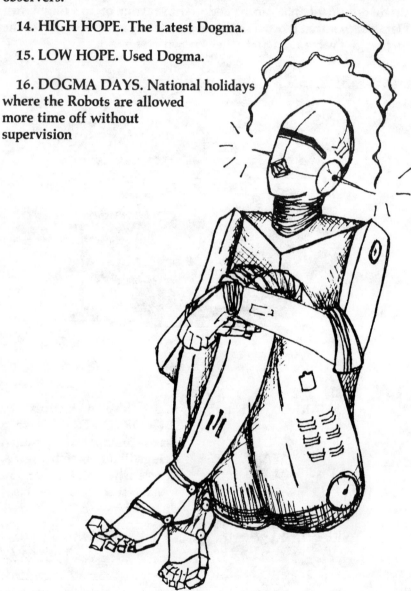

17. SLUMMING. Getting into a poor man's dogma.

18. DOGMA FARE. I will give you something for nothing if you will consume my dogma. Also known as politics.

LEX — — I — — CONS — · — PRESCRIPTIONS

I received a letter the other day from a man working for Dogma Control. This non-profit organ of an Un-namable religion, suggested that I participate in a chemical control program. They believe that chemicals are destroying the minds of your youth. I have reproduced my reply:

Dr. Wormly Willie White
Chemical Control Shelter
Born Again Road
Stifle Penn.

Dr. Dr. White:

Thank you for your letter asking me to head up your fine cause in my area. I am sorry but I must decline.

I am presently too busy working on my own salvation campaign. My work revolves around the fact that words change the chemical make-up of the micro-cells in the human brain. It has been proven many years ago, that all learning creates chemical as well as physical brain changes. The brain grows and changes micro-shapes as we learn. This is particularly true in infancy and childhood.

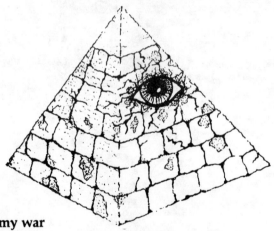

Therefore my war
on drugs takes the
shape of a war on words.
Words are chemicals -- as you read
this my words are changing the shape of your brain. You may wish to stop here, since who knows what the results might be. My research using brain scans and micro-photography indicates that children who are taught to hate themselves -- feel guilty and frightened -- repress their sexual drive have peculiar micro-brain patterns. The density of structure is different and less flexible than those children who do not learn the lessons of self-hate, repression and emotional violence.

You might ask about my sample, and as a scientist I am obliged to tell the truth. The brain damaged group consisted of 1000 units kidnapped randomly from various religious organizations across our country. The kidnapping took place during a chemical con job, that is during Sunday Services. The control group was carefully selected from the Garden Of Eros. The results indicate [probability of error 1 in 10 million], that those who attend Sunday Services have different micro-brain cell structures and composition than those that play in the Garden of Eros, and that this particular type of dogma is bad for your health. In my attempt to remedy this epidemic, I have taken it upon myself to set up DOGMA CONTROL CENTERS across the country.

In closing let me ask how you got my address and why did you write to me? You do know that we are on different sides? In courtesy, I will offer you a free week in our UNDOING CENTER. With enough hard work, I think we can get your brain back in shape.

Amen ----- Awomen. etc.etc.etc.

P.S. Have you ever tried the Lamed-Aleph position?

P.S.S. Be careful of what you read it might change your brain! BYE!BYE!

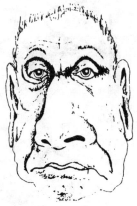

Prior to going to press, I received another letter from guess who? I am reproducing his letter and my reply. Let the reader decide which one of us makes more sense.

Dear Sir:

Your letter of the other day has just arrived at my office and at the suggestion of the Board of Directors of the Scared Scribes Of The Apostle Paul, I have been ordered to inform you, that your book as well as yourself have been placed on our List.

We are buying every copy of your book, and then burning them in our incinerator. We believe that "people," if you can be called that, like yourself are destroying the moral fiber of this country by advocating that people should and can change their Brain to follow their own True Will. We hope our actions will be sufficient to drive that point home.

In the name of our Lord,

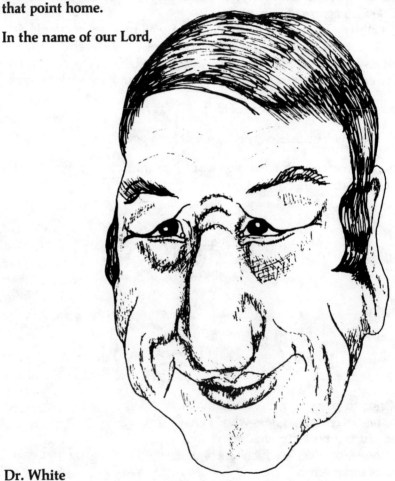

Dr. White

Dear Dr. White: **REPLY**

First let me ask a stupid question. What does moral fiber look like? Second, if you read my book thoroughly, you will remember that who-ever was closest to guessing the exact number of books sold would spend a weekend with the author. Well, I guess you win! You will find a Greyhound bus ticket and $25.00 expense money. Please give me a two-weeks notice so I may prepare your room. ETC., ETC.

As a result of this inter-change Dr. Wormly Willie White arrived at my home on Oct. 12. He spent a glorious weekend in the Sun. I showed him the Aleph-Lamed position and gave him a partner to work with. He now heads up our experimental alphabet center, and is presently working on the Resh-Yod position.

A question -- What in Dr. White's letter gave me the idea that I could UnDo him?

When all beauty dies,
so does man.

METHOD II

You should have practiced the first stage until you became aware of your deeper tensions. Before starting the second stage be sure your bladder, bowels, and stomach are empty.

LIE DOWN ON YOUR BACK

Take 10-15 deep breaths starting deep in your guts and work it upward. Try to become aware of all the muscles you use in breathing. When this has been done slowly get up. Stand straight up and count to three. When you reach three let the top part of your body collapse downward at your waist. Do not fall, just let it collapse, do not force it, let gravity pull it down. Repeat this 10-20 times. When you are finished take a few deep breaths and feel the effect this experiment had on you. See if you can sense your pelvic region. Now repeat the same experiment this time exhaling rapidly as you fall and breathing in slowly as you rise. Repeat this 10-20 times and then become aware of the sensations in your body.

LIE DOWN ON YOUR BACK

Inhale ----- as you do this slowly bring your legs with the knees flexed up to your chest, as you exhale kick your legs out as far and fast as you can. You might want to do this in bed or place some pillows under where your legs will fall. Repeat this until you start feeling tired, then allow your breathing to return to normal. When this happens start again but this time try to hold your legs extended for a second or two before you let them fall. Continue this for a minute or two and then relax again.

SENSE AND FEEL

Now inhale -- on the exhale scream — scream — scream, or if you are a male - yell -yell - yell. Repeat this at least five times. (In order to prevent your friends and neighbors from thinking you're nuts and phoning the police I suggest you yell or scream (depending on your sex, of course) into a pillow.

Now lie down on your back and sense and feel the energy moving around and throughout your body. Do this for about 5 minutes, and feel the life force move. When you are finished begin your mantram, or if you wish you may use the one recorded by Israel Regardie. If it is used following these experiments it will blow your mind. If you prefer to use your own, record it continually on a tape for at least 20 minutes and then play it back to yourself while you're meditating -- Method II is not meant to take the place of Method I, it is just an extension of the experiment. If you are inclined, make a note book or diary of your experiences. There are no-short cuts, so proceed seriously -- you can laugh at yourself later -- that is unless your laughter begins on its own. When you have completed this experiment try to spend at least ten to fifteen minutes alone. Don't eat or drink, just sense and feel.

CHAPTER FIVE

NEW ORGANS FOR EVERYONE
A HOPE —— A WISH —— A REALITY?

81

It is staggering -- [OH NO! There he goes again -- Breaking Set] -- to realize that as late as 1633, less than four hundred years ago, Galileo was hauled up before the Inquisition; there he was forced to recant his belief that the sun is the center of our solar system with the earth revolving about it, rather than vice versa. His abjuration was one of expediency for later he recanted his denial. He had long been a scientific heretic. While professor at the University of Pisa late in the sixteenth century he initiated experiments concerning the laws of bodies in motion.

These were contradictory to the teachings of Aristotle, the Greek philosopher whose theories, expounded in the fourth century B.C., still exert an incredible influence on the thinking of the Western World. Galileo's experiments and those of Copernicus opened a door into the scientific community through which some fresh ideas could flow. But so strongly entrenched was the teaching of Aristotle that most of us today, completely without our awareness, are still affected by his premises.

So rigid is the mental process that not until recent decades has his dogma been subjected to serious questioning. Even a slight examination of his premises will indicate the fallacy of the reasoning that for so many centuries has influenced scientific and philosophical thought — and indirectly the thinking processes of the man in the street.

This has also contributed to the reality in which we have been living, since beliefs do create our reality. Aristotle considered philosophy to be the discovery of certain self-evident, unchanging first principles that form the basis of all knowledge.

Yet today the Quantum Physicists declare that the very act of observing what we consider to be reality is sufficient to change it.

Even as we see or think or touch what is "outside" we organize "reality." The observer is such a vital part of the observed that we may never know anything but an alchemy, a Union of "out there" and ourselves.

The philosophy of Aristotle is as obsolete in today's world as a (You Fill in the Blank Space). Yet unfortunately his beliefs together with those of his teacher, Plato, continue to produce generations of people with Cave Mentality who live by Cave Logic.

CAVE MENTALITY MUST GO

One of Plato's most famous fables is the Myth of the Cave. We are looking at it now because of its accuracy when related to the world in which we live today. All too many of us are like prisoners in that cave which eternally faced away from the light.

They were unable to see themselves or anyone else because they were shackled with chains around their necks which prevented them from turning their heads. Above and behind them was a flickering fire and as men passed by the prisoners observed only the shadows cast against the wall; they refused to believe that reality was anything different from the shadows. Most of us are like prisoners in a mythical cave — -- prisoners shackled by Cave Logic: what mankind has always believed is true because it appears to be true. And by Cave Logic: what we think we see is reality because it looks real. We are unaware that we have been so programmed from infancy that what we see is what we have been taught to believe we are supposed to see. Consequently, like Robotic children — or like shackled slaves — most of us continue to see and believe what we are expected to see and believe.

IS IT DANGEROUS TO SEE

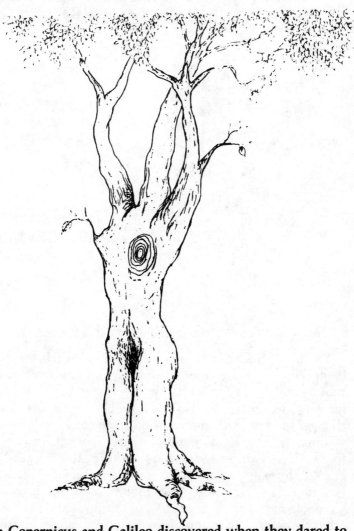

As both Copernicus and Galileo discovered when they dared to defy the dogmas of the Church, it is dangerous to be different; it is even more dangerous to see some TRUTH. All heretics before and since have discovered this all too

frightening fact.

—— CHANGE YOUR GLASSES ——
What Do You SEE?

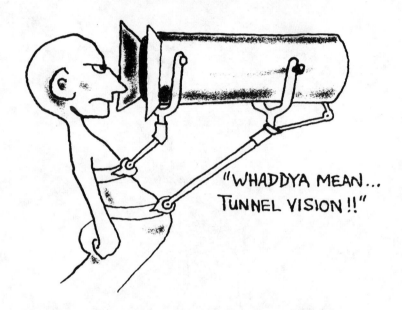

"WHADDYA MEAN...
TUNNEL VISION!!"

You have an edge on the mass of mankind. (Well, maybe.) You are being alerted to the changes that are coming upon mankind, so rapidly that Alvin Toffler has dealt with the speed of this change in his very informative *Future Shock*. It will be impossible to survive the change, to cope with the emotional, not to mention the physical trauma, without undergoing a drastic change in consciousness. (Note: Here again we see man as something that is pulled along, and changed by external forces. Do you like that image? Well, for most it is true.) The New Age will require new men, men of High Consciousness, and fortitude. All of our present dogma models will crumble before the vision of the immortal man who stands at the threshold. Those who would survive can do so only by grasping the vision of what lies ahead and beginning NOW to prepare to ride the crest of the New Wave that will carry them into an interesting future. But nature will no longer tolerate a rigid dragging foot. And the first step is to begin to UNDO yourself —— NOW.

WHAT DOES IT ALL MEAN MA—MEE

At this point we would like for you to pause a few minutes for a brief analysis that will help you to realize how conditioned all "your" opinions (I'm sorry I didn't mean to say your opinions, what I meant to say was every --- bo --- dy else's opinions are — — - about everything. Seated where you are now, lay your book down and look about you. Ask yourself ——— what does the chair I am sitting in mean? You will find that the chair has a host of associations which you have attributed to it which in reality have little to do with the chair itself. Now ask yourself:

What does this table mean?
What does this book mean?
What do my clothes mean?
What do my parents mean?
What do I mean?

Add some of your own questions to the list above. Let your eyes and your thoughts wander about the room you are sitting in, and then into other areas of your life and repeat the question. You will be amazed at how little your feeling or opinion about any object is related to the thing itself. It is based on a vast body of opinions, conditions, feelings and ideas that you have superimposed upon it, and which have very little relation to the object itself. Now let us try another experiment. It is advisable to spend considerable time — several minutes [Ha!] on each object — to make you aware of how conditioned you --- and --- not me --- are about everything in our lives. Look out the window and ask yourself as your eyes rest on each object, what is the truth about this tree, lawn, people walking on the street, or whatever your glance rests on? Mentally strip the objects to the facts that you perceive. Even your perception of what you believe to be facts concerning it or them is likely to be distorted -nevertheless your efforts to confine your conclusions to the apparent facts concerning it will help you to increase your awareness of how distorted are all our perceptions concerning everything in our lives. We rarely view anything without our fleshy robot machine being right in the middle. Almost all of our conclusions are based on "trained" input — which categorically means dogma.

Now we must begin to unlearn, to re-condition, to begin to change our consciousness and in the process change our lives, our immediate environment, and eventually contribute to changing the world itself. Be sure to give yourself sufficient time in the above exercises to become truly aware of this mis-conditioning all of us have been subjected to. Extend your glance and your thoughts into various areas of your life. Question certain conditions as well as various objects. It cannot be overemphasized that it is imperative to become aware of how we think if we are to change our consciousness. And thinking is such a rapid and subtle process that unless we take the time to examine our thinking processes we will continue to be unaware of how tricky and distorted are our perceptions.

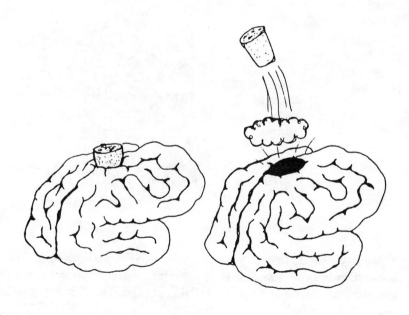

—— CHANGE YOUR BRAIN ——
What Do You Think?

OR
WAS DR. FRANKENSTEIN RIGHT AFTER ALL

Now we intend to help you see how much the past has contributed to your opinions. Again, it is imperative to give yourself adequate time to realize fully what you are thinking about an object, person or place. Ask yourself:

Because of the past when I see a (certain place) I think — -- Repeat with this:

(a certain person),
(a certain book),

[Take this book for example, a book elicits certain associations merely because it is a "book" -- I have intentionally made some errors in this book, have you noticed them yet? What errors were made intentionally? Which ones are merely mistakes? Or is the statement simply a device to cover up a sloppy job? Maybe all three statements are true? Maybe not? The answer is you don't know for sure. However the idea of breaking Set is the key. Have I broken your set yet? How many other explanations can you come up with in regards to the "errors" in this book? I am offering a reward of $50.00 for the person closest in guessing the number and location of my intentional errors, and the meanings of the --- internal code.].

(a certain face), etc.

Add other comparisons of your own. Very shortly you will be amazed to realize that it is you who have given meaning to each of the objects, conditions or people in question. You might realize that your thoughts have very little meaning, very little accuracy. And that you see very little if anything without your own personal conditioning and dogma *rearing* its ugly face. You will learn what an important factor Time plays in your life. You will learn that you rarely if ever live in the NOW — that you are always being dragged down by the burdens of your past and cluttering up your future with

the garbage of your associations. All this has to go. YOU HAVE TO GO. You must wipe the old slate clean. It has no place in the unborn future — no place in the Life of —— a real you, who will be swept into a new Wave of Life surging in the bowels of this planet.

To help (Can you tell when the author is really trying to help? Can you tell when he is just filling up space? Or is he full of shit, just trying to sell books? Why does he use so many styles? Name them.) at this point let us relate this habit of having the past drag us behind to some far more important aspects of your life. Now I want you to imagine that you are a Man from Mars. When you have created this image answer the questions below as honestly and as clearly as possible. Answer them as if there were no consequences for the TRUTH.

I like/dislike my job because
[No bullshit please.]

I like/dislike my neighbor because

I like/dislike my parents because
[No lies]

I married my spouse because?

Above all do not escape your answers with guilt, shame or cliches. Yet another experiment will prove to you how much of what you feel is unrelated to the person/place/condition/or thing you relate to. In the same manner as in the previous experiments, look at the following questions and apply them to various conditions in your life.

This person disturbs/enthralls me because
This place enthralls/disturbs me because
This condition disturbs/enthralls me because
This thing enthralls/disturbs me because

LIMITED SUPPLY PHILOSOPHY

You are likely to find that in one way or another the majority of your answers have been influenced, whether directly or indirectly, by the Limited Supply Dogma which has pervaded the Earth for **uncounted***(How much is the author like the book? Does he live what he preaches? What scares him? Which style is most like his basic personality? Would you like to meet him? What does he look like? Does he smoke cigars? Is he married?)***millenia.**

Basic to this philosophy was the limited life-span, with its eternal cycle of beginnings and endings. But now with reams of evidence that death itself will be conquered, the very foundation on which this philosophy rests is being cut to the quick. The Limited Supply and mortal philosophy is so deeply ingrained that conscious acts of re-programming are absolutely essential. Keep in mind that the very fact of the mortality concept is limiting. What could be more basic to the idea of limitation than a limited number of years to live? The artificial and arbitrary standards of evaluation which have been placed on you by the Establishment -- the term of service with a company, marriage, your status in the community, your financial statement, etc. But in an Unlimited Life of Limitless Supply such standards of evaluation are utterly non-sensical. If life never ends there is no end point for evaluation and judgment. As sta-$$-ndards change so will the mind and visa versa. There will be nothing to fight for because even if accumulation is your personal goal, your time will be infinite. All pressure will be removed. Those who still desire ultimate power will have less clout with which to influence you because you will be independent of them.

Scare tactics based on death and restriction become useless once the limited supply philosophy becomes obsolete. In a world of unlimited supply, power structures and leaders as we know them today will be totally useless. This could well be the one reason that funds and efforts are *limited* for unlimited supply research. [*Is the author paranoid when he makes references to intentional plots to control the minds and bodies of people? If so why? If not what evidence can you think of?*]

Entrenched authority is not likely to look with favor on research which will end its mindless control over our minds and body. When UNLIMITED SUPPLY becomes a reality the Alexanders, Napoleons, Hitlers, and less obvious lunatics will have to change their strategy. The search for Immortality must never be left in the dirty hands **(Do politicians wash their hands more than non-politicians?)** of political-government-corporate cartels.

Dear Mom:

Without you and all the silly people who
wanted someone else to run their lives I
couldn't have done it.

Your loving son,

N

P.S. Right now I really don't have time to
give you a grandchild.

Unlimited supply and immortality is iconoclastic to all present forms of Mind-Body control. It is terrifying to conceive of the results

if the secret of immortality were wholly theirs. If everyone could achieve immortality all present forms of power would melt away.

There would be no need for power structures; only if they had a monopoly on immortality could they offer anything which you could not better negotiate for yourself. Should they manage to obtain such a monopoly their grasp on your mind and body would intensify the sense of meaninglessness and purposelessness that already plagues the majority of mankind.

The unlimited supply philosophy will change all our attitudes. Since time will then be limitless, whether or not one acquires or achieves something "right now" will no longer be as important as it is now. [*We will no longer be driven, but instead be driving.*] There will always be a legion of Tomorrows in which to reach the desired goal. Instead of the compulsive drive for acquisition there will then be a new sense of freedom, a timelessness. To the un -- initiated mind this could create a sense of meaninglessness, but to the en -- lightened mind it would mean true freedom to follow the Will. Dis-ease as we know it will disappear. Intelligence will increase and the limited supply value system full of paranoia will disintegrate. The need for childish religions will be replaced by JOY experiences rather than fear motivated behaviors. Such experiences would become the Purpose and Power of man as he became involved with the true search for Union with his Higher life -- without -- having to give up his body unless he decided to trade it in.

CHANGE IS THE ONLY CONSTANT

"AMERICAN SUBURBAN SURVIVALISTS"

If such ideas seem strange, perhaps impossible, we would remind you that Life is in a constant state of flux. History records man's perceptions of the "truth" and these perceptions are firmly distorted, as anyone knows who has researched historical sources.

On the other hand Legend and Myth preserve the essence of the truth. This is validated by the similarity of world legends that persist in all parts of the world and in all cultures and religions. One of these is the Legend of Atlantis, and from it we can learn much that is pertinent to the global house-cleaning forthcoming in the immediate future. Nature, which normally seems to move with the speed of a slightly paralyzed snail, appears at times to decide to go forward in great comet-like bursts of speed. At such times woe be it to laggards. They are trampled in the rush to escape.

Legend tells us that when it was time for the great continent of Atlantis to become submerged beneath the ocean, those of its inhabitants who were alert, aware and tuned in -- were in some "miraculous" fashion whisked safely to other parts of the globe. And so they were able to escape the catastrophe that overtook their fellow beings.

Nature is once again sending out warning signals galore. Among them is the proliferation of centers for consciousness expansion. There are New Age teachers, such as Bob Anton Wilson, and Tim Leary, (who have been strongly influenced by Mr. Crowley and his Student Israel Regardie who provided the "bridge", the integrating factor between mysticism and science. For those who didn't know Francis Regardie personally, at the age of 75 he was as open to new experiences as a young adult. While age took its toll, he never became obsolete, rigid or fixated. I wish all of us could follow his example.) Those who refuse to read and be guided accordingly, like the ancient Atlanteans, will be overwhelmed in the catastrophic days ahead. (How do you like that threat?) But those of you who choose to become undone and enlightened will be guided and protected. (How do you like that promise?)

They will be Nature's Super Race that now stands impatiently in the wings awaiting its cue to come on stage. If we are to survive, the first necessity is to change both our attitudes and our perceptions.

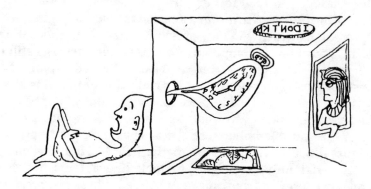

As Gary Zukau points out in the *Dancing Wu Li Masters*, atoms are "Hypothetical entities constructed to make experimental observations intelligible." Yet for so long have we dealt with the idea of an atom that we completely forget it is simply that — an idea. And even when we deal with the idea of an atom we are in reality dealing with something which is largely non-existent. An atom consists of a complex arrangement of electrons revolving around a nucleus composed of protons — positively charged particles, and neutrons —uncharged particles.

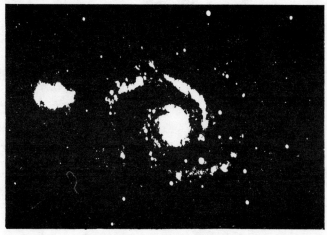

It has been said that if the nucleus of an atom were the size of a pea which had been placed on the 50 yard line of a sports stadium, the rest of its parts, the electrons, would be spinning at the top of the grandstand. This gives you an idea of the amount of empty space within the electron shell forming the perimeter of the atom.

This being the case, turn your attention to your body. Now decide if the opinions which you may previously have held about it have validity. Your body is composed of atoms — for scientists still use the term in describing material objects. Therefore your body consists of mostly empty space. It is a collection of whirling atomic particles, temporarily held in place for the lifetime of the body.

And yet the British physicist, Sir Arthur Eddington says, "the stuff of the world is mind stuff," because as the modern physicist continues his search he finds not matter in stasis, but vital energy. "The material universe begins to look like a fantastic cosmic interplay of energy and consciousness." Already Physics is speculating that mind can and will move matter and shape it into other forms. Dr. William A. Tiller, Professor of Material Science and Engineering at Stanford states, "A biological transformation to another sensory system appears to be taking place in humanity at this time." More and more scientists are beginning to give validity to the hypothesis of the metaphysicists. That while we are accustomed to using the terms life and death as if they were true opposites, this is a grave mistake. They are finding that the only opposites are Birth and Death for "life is a constant unending Continuum."

(Hell! I'd rather have
some of that old time religion,
wouldn't you?)

LOOK OUT THROUGH
ACCORDION EYES

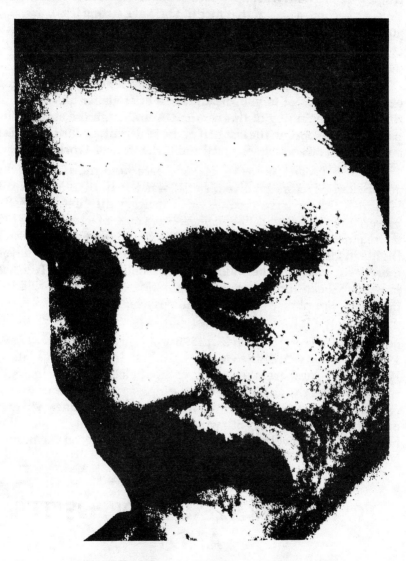

"That statement sounds quite paranoid."

Wake up! See the writing on the wall! Stretch your vision! OUCH! As a current TV commercial states, The Future Is Here Now. Get with it! Realize —— THAT THE PURPOSE OF LIFE IS TO CHANGE IT! No longer will mankind be permitted to perpetuate a troglodyte mentality. A super-race of super-WoMen is on the way. You can become a part of that race (if you have strong legs), or if not you can putter along in your accustomed nightmare until NATURE stamps you OBSOLETE and tosses you out among the Rejects. *(If reason doesn't work try scare tactics.)*

If you still question the exponential change that is now occurring everywhere (except in your head) take a brief glance backwards in time to the beginning of this century. And though the automobile had been developed in the last half of the 19th century the country as a whole was not on wheels until about the time of World War I.

Leonardo as early as 1514 sketched a parachute and discussed the aerodynamic factors involved. But it was not until 1903 that the Wright Brothers were credited with making the first successful powered airplane flight. The airplane was a minor factor in WWI but it remained for Charles Lindbergh to pioneer the way for transoceanic flights in 1927. Then in 1969 the United States landed two (maybe more) astronauts on the Moon. The possibility of such a feat had previously been limited to the imagination of writers of science-fiction; (a nice phrase for stark raving psychotics).

Jules Verne wrote *From the Earth to the Moon* in 1865. H.G. Wells published *The War of the Worlds* in 1898 and *The First Man on the Moon* in 1901. Edison invented the electric light bulb in 1879 but as late as WWII many rural areas were still without electricity. A moment's reflection over the above figures, relating them to the thousands of millenia which preceded them in the history of the planet will give one a clue as to the speed with which Nature is suddenly accelerating her plans for the evolution of the race. (Put 11 bucks on the nose of Mother Nature). The time is at hand:

TO RECONCILE THE OPPOSITES
AND
EXTEND THE LIGHT

To throw off these clothes and these naked bones —to leave my emotions in the dust — to cast my mind into the darkness of space — burning my habits in the demon's fire. When this is done, falling blindly into the abyss -- only then do I begin.

THIS IS BRAIN CHANGE WILLED HISTORICALLY KNOWN AS MAGICK

METHOD III

Again Method III is not meant to take the place of Method I or II, but is a further extension of the technique. This will take a little more time and you shouldn't try this until you have mastered and documented the effects of the other two methods.

STAND UP

Bend your knees slightly, not too much and let the top part of your body flop forward. Do not force it -- just let it drop.

While you're in this position, use a five count breath. Five in, hold five, five out, hold five. Repeat this three times and slowly straighten yourself out. Repeat this sequence 08 times or more. When you're done, stand erect for a few moments with your eyes tightly shut. Become aware of any tension in your face, neck or shoulders. Mobilize these tensions by opening your mouth as wide as you can and distorting your face. Now close your mouth and continue on with these distortions. When you've done this for at least 5 minutes, bend your head back on your shoulders as far as you can, and start turning it from side to side. Some people might get nauseous at this point, so be prepared. If by some chance you desire to vomit go right ahead, since the gag reflex is marvelous for reducing deep body tension.

GETTING OUT OF YOUR HEAD

Sit down again and think about something which you are worried about. Get up again and pace around the room repeating the phrase, "Wh -- ats go -- ing to hap -- pen to me," or some equivalent phrase which expresses worry. Try not to numb yourself while you are doing this. If you feel silly that's fine, because your worry --- ing is silly anyway. Now after five minutes sit down in your chair and think of something joyful. When you have it in mind get up and pace around the room repeating the phrase, "I love it," or some equivalent phrase expressing happiness or joy. When your five minutes are up, imitate laughter as well as you can, then tears, alternating these emotions for at least five minutes. When you are done lie down.

Clasp your hands over your chest, pull your knees up and roll yourself up as tight as you can in a ball, tensing every muscle. Hold this position for at least three minutes. Feel your restrictions, now expand, let go of your restriction, let go of everything. As you start to expand let out a shout such as AH! Become aware of your freedom. Repeat this a few times.

MEDITATE

Choose your mantram, or point of focus, and begin your meditation.

SUGGESTIONS

There are many ways to use these and the more advanced techniques. Do not become rigid in your experiments — yet remain diligent in your efforts. Some people do better by alternating levels, i.e. use Method I on Monday, II on Wednesday, and III on Saturday, then switch Methods and Days the following week. Others stay with one Method for one month and then switch to others. Be open with your experiments but always remain dedicated to the work. During these periods of experimentation, call yourself by different names, this will help separate the machine you from the emerging Self — the true Scientist of the LAB. If you have any difficulties or questions or wish to find out more information, please feel free to drop me a short note.

CHAPTER SIX AND ONE HALF

RESULTS

We are near the end of this work. By now you should have established your LAB. I suggest that you keep its location secret, since there are many "out there" who might think you're crazy if you don't act like a dopey robot. With proper security your LAB will be free of unwanted inter-fear-ence.

THERE IS NO NEED TO BE PARANOID

For those of you who can't wait for my next book in the Undoing Yourself Series, may I advise the study of Tantra Yoga, hypnosis, (see Steven Heller's *Monsters and Magical Sticks — There's No Such Thing As Hypnosis?*) operant conditioning techniques, and Magic as elucidated by Israel Regardie's classic work *The Complete Golden Dawn System of Magic*, and if you're really brave Crowley's *Gems From The Equinox*, introduced by Israel Regardie. Of course the source for these books is —— Falcon Press.

If you still don't know who I was referring to in the LAB section, his name is Master Therion, or Aleister Crowley. We of the LAB are greatly indebted to the courage and genius of this HERO, who was unjustly degraded and vilified by SYMONDS and the Paul —— ian Press — not that he was perfect — thank GOD — who needs a perfect hero? For a deeper understanding of A.C. read Israel Regardie's *Eye in the Triangle.*

SIRIUS OR OTHERWISE

If you have not decided how to take this work and require a decision, take the work seriously, since certain sections were written with that intention. On the other hand, since most people do not change their life based on what they read, regard the whole thing as a joke on someone — you — me — the publishers — Crowley —or the book distributors.

For those STUDENTS who practice these techniques with dedication we believe that you will in fact become your own LAB and EXPERIMENTER, which if you haven't guessed yet means *Magick* or "Brain Change Willed."

The truth of Becoming more than HUMAN, the goal of all legitimate occult and psychological systems, is nothing more than becoming your own LAB and EXPERIMENTER, intentionally changing your brain and chemistry to meet your "desired" (TRUE WILL) ends.

THE THIRD SECTION

THE NEW POLYTHEISM
OF BROTHERS/SISTERS
WHAT IS THE SCORE?
TEN LAWYERS TO ONE ENGINEER

THE WHO'S
WHO
OF
THE WHO
GOD IS DEAD
THE GODS ARE BORN

FUTANT MUTANTS
THE MANY IN THE ONE

Job Descriptions Below

If you resolved to study the obvious and the unique you may have just wandered onto the path of the Futant Mutant.
C.S. Hyatt, Ph.D. Zen Buddhist Priest, The New Western School

Know Thy Self Is The Great Lie
Know Thy Selfs Is The Great Truths
Mono-Brain Vs. Poly-theistic Brains

Nietzche said, "For the individual to set up his own ideal and derive from it his laws, his pleasures, and his rights that has perhaps been hitherto regarded as the most monstrous of all human aberrations, and as idolatry in itself; in fact, the few who have ventured to do this have always needed to apologize. It was the marvelous art and capacity for creating Gods, in polytheism, that this impulse was permitted to discharge itself, it was here that it became purified, perfected, and ennobled.

"Monotheism, on the contrary, the rigid consequence of the doctrine of one normal human being, consequently the belief in a normal God, beside who there are only false, spurious Gods, has perhaps been the greatest danger of mankind in the past. In polytheism man's free-thinking and many-sided thinking has a prototype set up: the power to create for himself new and individual eyes, always newer and more individualized."

When discussing monotheism is Nietzche anticipating that our problem in being human is in fact the problem of the illusion of singularity? In particular is our philosopher commenting on the idea of the One Self -- One Body Illusion? Is he aware of the Buddhist idea of no-Self (impermanence -- Dukkha -- sorrow)?

Does he see the transformation of society occuring from a New Polytheism? A Sister/Brother Cult?

Has he even performed a greater leap and sensed that polytheism really correlates with multiple brain(s) models of the universes? Has he anticipated the notion that culturalization is simply the channelization for a preference of a singular brain mode activity, like the overly-simplified right/left brain model? Is he stating that culture is merely a form of advanced toilet training?

Is his call that God is dead, really the calls that the Gods are being born, that we are beginning to learn that the notion of an "I" is an illusion, a legal convention predicated on slavery and not an existential fact?

Is he telling us that we are many brains and personalities and that the notion of split personalities as an illness is a lie, and the notion of one self is truly the dis-ease? Is he aware that much of our unnecessary pain is the result of trying to make all of us breathe as one?

Does he know that schizophrenia is really the result of not paying adequate attention to our multiplicity? Is its rigid attitude an attempt to unify, make a whole of something which is not a whole to begin with?

We will find out that Undoing Yourself is another phrase for God Is Dead, the final obituary of stupidity, the end of the single brain -- the single self -- the freedom from restrictions, the new Nirvana(s). Undoing Yourself is the Religions of Sisters/Brothers.

As we examine the world of multiple brains and correlation matrices, we will be struck by the idea that the worlds and the personalities are not unitary, but instead are touching circles which forever change their centers as new and more dynamic INFO WARPS are added. In other words we are dealing with shifting centers and expanding peripheries.

Each human factor or brain function operates according to its own rules. Thus our sense of unity is simply a sense, a moment of integration. Our sense of wholeness, comes about through living and exploring each fragment, without forcing a single principle onto the process. Thus in muddling toward enlightenments we begin to hear the voices of all the Gods and Goddesses, serving each in our own ways.

WHO EVER HAS THE ULTIMATE POWER TO DEFINE HAS THE ULTIMATE POWER ALL SELF FULFILLING PROPHECIES ARE SELF FULFILLING YOU CAN'T BE BORN AGAIN WHEN THERE IS NO YOU

In the book The Intelligence Agents by Timothy Leary, Ph.D. (Falcon Press, 1988 revised and updated edition) there still remains a piece entitled "Beware of Monotheism." This piece predates much of the work on the dangers of monotheism, whether it lies in the family, the corporation, the healing arts, the state, education, etc. What it does not emphasize is that monotheism is the PRIMARY FACTOR accounting for most human misery. For those familiar with factor analysis, Monotheism and its derivate Mono†Mania, singular causality, etc. has the highest loading of any factor. It accounts for most of our behavior, values, ideas, confusions, misery, and feelings.

To quote:

"Monotheism is the primitive religion which centers human consciousness on Hive Authority. There is One God and His Name is ------- (substitute Hive-Label).

"If there is only One God then there is no choice, no option, no selection of reality. There is only Submission or Heresy. The word Islam means 'submission'. The basic posture of Christianity is kneeling. Thy will be done.

"Monotheism therefore does no harm to hive-oriented terrestrials (Stages 10, 11, and 12) who eagerly seek to lay-off responsibility on some Big Boss. [Note: I disagree with the notion of no-harm].

"Monotheism does profound mischief to those who are evolving to post-hives stages of reality. Advanced mutants (Stages 13-18) do make the discovery that 'All is One' as the realization dawns that, 'My Brain creates all the realities that I experience.' [Note: substitute **brains** and All is still All].

"The discovery of Self is frightening because the novitiate possessor of the Automobile Body and the Automobile Brain must accept all the power that the hive religious attributed to the jealous Jehovah.

"The First Commandment of all Monotheism is: I am the Lord, they God: Thou shalt have no other Gods before me. All monotheisms are vengeful, aggressive, expansionist, intolerant. . .

"It is the duty of a monotheist to destroy any competitive heresy. Concepts such as devil, hell, guilt, eternal damnation, sin, evil are fabrications by the hive to insure loyalty to Hive Central. All these doctrines are precisely designed to intimidate and crush individualism . . ." [Note: the notion of many individuals is equivalent to polytheism.].

A Word of Caution To the Third Section

This book has been written for only 64 people. In order to reach them we have published and distributed this book throughout the world. I hope this act does not offend the 64.

DEATH AND STUPIDITY -- THE HISTORY OF MONOMANIA

There are two enemies which mankind may not recover from. Number one is Stupidity: I place this before death since the amelioration of stupidity is necessary before death can be conquered.

The DNA GODDESSES has us scheduled for a bright future. However, its scheduling is based on the law of discomfort. This law states that man usually does not embark on dangerous and difficult ventures unless he is motivated. Thus the wo/man of the hour, the consort of DNAS, are those who know how to use discomfort to discover great truths. Discomfort is simply the emergence of a new Goddess. It is birth of a new center which in time will become a periphery.

AIDS

Motivation is frequently pain, misery and fear. It is the Dukkha from which we all try to escape. AIDS is an example. This epidemic that could destroy us all, has motivated Man to spend money, time and effort on research. It may even create a sense of world unity. Some like the fundamentalists believe that AIDS is a curse or punishment: however, it may turn out to be something like a reward.

Their view is singular and based on the ideations of monotheism, (the one law), a one brain function psycho-philosophy of cave dwellers.

Research on AIDS may help us see through the genetic window which may lead to immortality, the enemy of heaven/hell theorists.

POT LUCK

DNAS are designed to maintain status quo until the time is right for change. This relates to the notion of monotheism and Poly-Brain—Theism, the serving of the various Neuro-Gods. This happens by pot luck.

Pot luck occurs when apparently orderly systems proceed normally until they reach a critical point and become chaotic. A switch from brain focus 'A' to brain focus 'B'. In other words when we have taken a God to an extreme, chaos begins. At that point another Goddess emerges.

Chaos does not mean randomness in the normal sense of the word. What it means is that linear equations (monotheisms) are no longer operative and predictions based on them temporarily collapse. After a period of time of observing these "random" events, a new principle emerges. (Note: this idea is not similar to the 100th Monkey model which has now been discredited.)

Some scientists have used notions of "initial sensitivity" as a model to understand types of pot luck. In other words, a minor or even an unnoticed event in the beginning of an activity may show up near the end as a gigantic discrepancy. This applies to throwing dice as well as the quality of neonate which emerges from the womb.

THE MENTAL CROTCH OF POLY—CONSCIOUSNESS

Stupidity is the refusual to leave the present track, or re-interpret data that does not conform to the present linear model, (the present Goddess).

Immortality would destroy much of OUR beliefs and allow us to break from the present linear model of monotheism.

The GODS are sending signals that some of us are ready for the changes that immortality and reduced stupidity would bring. Conclusion: Score -- Genetic engineers 15 -- Lawyers 1.

At present immortality research is not a high priority for governments and groups who are possessed by notions of afterlife and have accepted death as a standard and in some cases a DESIRED standard. Our understanding of Death is based on our monotheism, the serving of One Slave God now and forever more.

THE NECESSARY MOTHERS

Necessity and pure curiosity are the mothers of poly-gods. The idea of womb and mothering are very important concepts. The births of the Gods follows an interesting pattern of:

THE URGE, THE FERTILIZATION, THE INCUBATION, THE GIVING BIRTH, THE NURTURING.

You will note that there are at least two convulsive-chaotic periods in this creative process. Also there are at least two waiting or boring periods, commonly known as routines. However, the entire process adds up to five and not four. In other words sleeping within each "□completed state□" there lurks the serpent of disruption.

WORLD UNREST IS THE RESULT
OF A GRAND IDEA BEING BORN
THE TERROR MONOTHEISTS FEEL IS BIRTH PANGS

Ideas can be very painful to the creators. A new idea is the result of the dethroning of a reigning God.

WE ARE ALL HEXAGRAMS

I am looking for 64 brave human nervous systems who have the intelligence and resources to create an Undoing Yourself Vessel, dedicated to research on personal and transpersonal problems from the point of view of sister/brother polytheism. Please send your resume at once! No Jokes! Score is Unknown.

THE MUDDLED CLASS
THE SCHIZOPHRENIA OF MONOTHEISM
THE □ 4 G'S □
ALL CLASS STRUCTURE DISSOLVES WITH MOTION

The middle class, or as I refer to them, the muddled class, are known by their life/death stance for the 4 G's. They are Gravity **worship**, Geography **worship**, Genetics **worship**, and Genius negative **worship**. The attentive reader will note the similarity between worship and warship. War is the result of worshipping the 4 G's.

The 4 G's or the □Box of Life□ proceeds the □†□Box of Death† by an unspecified number of years. Again note the 4's. The muddled class strives for the illusion of perfect □order□.

The muddled class has the uncanny ability to turn hope into fear, potency into impotency. They are eternally perplexed in legitimatizing everything through a process known as trance-duction. (See Monsters and Magical Sticks, Falcon Press, 1987).

Power needs are really the desire to serve. Sex is really love. Dogma and stupidity are personal preferences. Getting drunk is wine tasting. Ritual is spontaneity. Genetic selfishness (reproduction) is Planned Parenthood. Opinions are intuitions. A □box□ is really a home. Intellectualism is wisdom. Confusion is intelligence. Sin is mental illness. Status seeking is good taste. Possessions are antiques.

One sure sign of muddle-dumb, is the need to make all diversity into □□□□□□Unity□□□□. All uniqueness into sameness. It is the philosophy of the One God. Score -- Lawyers 14 -- Engineers 1

THE FIRST TWO G'S EXPLAINED

The First G -- Gravity: Weight and Mass: Density: The bearing of the weight of the One God. The muddled class measures themselves by the amount of weight they have accumulated.

Weight is conventionally known as possessions. The measure of the worth of these possessions is the amount of dust they collect. It is the world of the Hoover and Pledge. [J.E. & Allegiance]

Gravity is viewed economically as stability. That is, the more you weigh, the harder it is to move. Thus banks are willing to lend you more money to buy more things which in turn makes you more stable. This in turn makes you a better risk.

Location, in time/space, is a monotheistic gravity absolute which has dire economic consequences for those who wish to move around (Poly-neural philosophers).

Freedom to move about is a status symbol of both the wealthy and the wise. Score -- Polytheists 23 Lawyers 0

GEOGRAPHY

I use the term geography (lines dividing time and space on a piece of paper) to refer to culture and psychology. Psycho-culture is the result of genes interacting with geography.

In a primitive sense, culture and psychology are territory. We act as if we are the primary creators of our personality, our attitudes, beliefs, and values.

Although gravity limits the types of cultures/psychologies we can have, there is a sufficient array to warrant the notion of psycho-culture-god relativism. This notion has started an international conflict. Everyone is taking pride in their own personal brand of stupidity.

CULTURE IS SURELY FOR BACTERIA

Americans can eat oysters but shy away from snails.
The French love snails but dislike locusts.
Zulus munch on locust but avoid fish.
Jews eat fish but avoid pork.
Hindus eat pork but worship beef.
Russians love beef but hate snakes.
Chinese devour snakes but not people.
The Jale of New Guinea find people delightful -- to eat.

WARS ARE WARS BETWEEN SLAVES

All wars are wars between slaves. Each competing hoard of geo-slaves believes that its form of slavery is better. A country by any other name is - - - a choice between serfdoms. Each bible, is simply a slave's survival manual or HOW TO book!

WHERE LIVES THE STRAIGHT LINE LURKS THE CURVES

One purpose of chaos, paradox, nonsense, and absurdity is to set itself against the linear world. These are not meant to take the place of linear knowledge or functions, but to act as a point of focus calling our attention and awareness to the something(s) which the linear model has missed, thus breathing new life into the predictable.

Further, our non-linear models help us to see old facts in new and exciting ways. If there is a summum bonum it lies in reformulation and utility in the service of tolerating more of the unknown.   The function of Monotheism is to control the anxiety created by the unknown. Monotheism is a form of glue which attempts to hold an expanding world together.

However, to view these models as truths eternal leads to the possibility of destruction now facing us. For example, Veblen thought that it was easier for society to regress than advance. For Veblen, this regression might lead back to a society characterized by smallness, co-operation, peacefulness, and hard work, rather than the industrialized barbarism which he felt existed in his time (1857-1929). Many new-agers, agriculturalists, and religionists might favor this. I do not.

Ogburn felt that doctrine always lagged behind innovation. This idea may lead to pocket societies within a larger society. This is particularly true if knowledge and information are accelerating as many believe. However, this is not entirely pessimistic, particularly if we all learn to let other people live in their own dogmas without having to reform them violently. However, some dogmas feel that other dogmas are a danger to them and in this vein feel justified in acting violently. The answer is to remove the police power from all dogmas. In other words, create a police force like the one in The Day The Earth Stood Still. Polytheism 10, Engineers 20, Lawyers 1

Those of us who are trying to live outside popular dogmas appear to dogmatists to be more powerful than we believe. Most of modern day evangelism believes we are worthy of fighting against. We are a force to be dealt with. The Goddess(es) has made her move. However, the move is laden with danger and excitement. We have to begin to use our hearts and our heads.

The whole damm thing, remember is about emancipation, not just for a race, but for the whole human race. We need to emancipate ourselves from our cultural givens, such as the bio-social man-dates concerning reproduction.

In this author's view reproduction is of the greatest concern, not just in terms of physical resources, but in terms of mental resources. We cannot afford to lose too many minds to the reproduction Wo/Man/date (Reproduce and Die). This has been the primary method-purpose of religions and societies, insuring the continuation of slaves-workers hypnotized into stupidity. However, the job is done. There are enough of us!. The entire process of procreation and child-rearing needs a new twist. Take a turn into the future -- go for quality and for-ever. The days of quantity, the sacrifices to the hungry God are dying. Let us bury it along with our bestial ideologies which are the property of the dead. Inherit information and wisdom!

ONE PART OF THE BRAINS
IS ALWAYS AHEAD OF THE OTHERS
MODEL MASTERS
THE INFINITE CORRELATION MATRICES
OEDIPUS SCHMEDIPUS AS LONG AS YOU LOVE YOUR MOTHER
THE THERAPY OF HYATT -- COMPASSION AND DATA

Below is an elementary form of the subjective correlation matrix of a human brains, struggling with the Oedipus Myth. Dr. Freud, a new age computer programmer was one of the first to have a glimpse into the correlation matrices of the brains. He used the free association technique to try to understand the connections.

THE EXPERIENCE: Young brains/body is lying next to its caretaker, an older female-brains-body, known by the ideology as "mother". Young-brains/body, a male-younger-brains-body, is known in ideology as "baby". As the two year old baby lies and rubs next to mother there is a feeling of pleasure all over the brains/body including the area know ideologically as the sex-organs. The baby rubs more and more and experiences more and more sensation know ideologically as "pleasure". This is variable Y, sensation.

Variable X is female, caretaker, mother. Variable Z is situation, lying in bed, rubbing. Correlations for these variables are now at a theoretical = 1.00. Score Life 100 -- Lawyers 0

IDEOLOGY: The young brains(s) goes to church at the age of 7 years old and learns from an ideological hack that something called incest is evil. YB (young brains) has no idea what this means, except that the entire experience is associated with sitting still, being quiet, adulting, and loud noises. Quite complicated? Not at all! Ok, I will go on.

As a good primate YB attempts to imitate the adults, but as a good primate YB fails, and is chastised by the larger female caretaker (FB).

Correlations are now mixed and varied.

At age ten YB is lying in bed with FB rubbing and enjoying when FB senses that something is wrong, and rejects the rubbing behavior. YB is in conflict since the correlation of 1 is losing ground. There is pain, loud noises which are associated with other loud noises. The adults are upset. YB is told that this type of behavior is no-longer appropriate. YB doesn't understand whether it is the feeling, the behavior, the situation or him which is unacceptable.

Scene switches back to church, this time YB gets a sense of what incest means, "pleasure with a member of your family". This has something to do with bodily pleasure. It is evil and you will go to hell. Numerous correlations have been established among these ideologies, experiences and conclusions. YB is now in conflict and searching for a solution which more often then not will be only partial and in error. He might think, "I am bad, I have a secret to keep, She knows, Does he (MB-father) know, does the preacher know?"

A state of anxiety ensues as previous correlations begin to break apart. The YB has a number of options of which I will mention just two. Compartmentalize the first experience, that is keep it separate from the other data and correlations, or integrate it, even though it makes no sense, into a predesigned ideology. Remember who ever has the ultimate power to define, has the ultimate power.

One ideology that might work is that men are evil, he is man, therefore he is evil and he will do evil things which can be Undone by going to confession. This ideology allows him to keep some of the correlations intact, by simply accepting that he is inherently bad, should feel bad, and can ease the pain by performing certain rituals.

Evilness now becomes a factor. We might view a factor as something which accounts for the variability in the world. It might be called an explanatory construct, even though it is an ideological definition. Evilness is simply a garbage pail factor. A place to put things which terrify YB.

As time goes on YB matures, marries, and raises his own family, but suffers from various dis-eases such as ulcers. He decides to go to psychoanalysis for treatment. The analyst attempts to locate highly emotionally laden correlation matrices. After some time a set is found and the analyst helps YB face this set of correlations in terms of the analyst's ideology which might be that man struggles between good and evil, life and death, sex is pleasure, his wife is not his mother, he must not touch his daughters sex organs, etc. YB feels better, his ulcer disappears and the analyst believes that his definitions, world view, and methods are validated. In other words YB's is socialized and the analyst's theories are redeemed.

Suffice it to say that our correlation matrices are complicated and interwoven not just conceptually, but emotionally, and sensorially. It is a difficult task to find them and re-correlate since our sense(s) of our self(s) is built on them.

UNDOING YOURSELF METHOD
POLY—THEISTIC "THERAPIES"

I have developed a method combining, energized meditation, computer analysis of language and sensorial preference, compassion, confrontation and a process known as 'empty out' to locate deep correlations which prevent individuals from actualizing their own true wills. These methods help to uncorrelate and re-correlate data which is now unproductive for making life work.

With our poly-theistic approach we begin to search for experiences, conclusions and ideologies which have been used to □crate□ a world view. We begin to take them apart, creating a multiple world view. We search for conflict and false resolutions. We employ the sensorium, multiple brain methods and behavior to achieve a shift in the mono-maniacal model which causes the person unnecessary pain. We begin to locate and develop resources which are unknown productive correlations.

Information is always being correlated at multiple levels and requires an in depth method to examine the processes and conclusions involved.

Our correlation matrices (CM) can be very useful if we learn how to access them. Dreams are one way, sensory deprivation another. A technique I employ with individuals working with restricted CMS is to temporarily deprive them of the use of one of their senses. This is especially useful with individuals who have correlated certain emotions with specific ritualized and feared behaviors. These individuals have been taught that emotions and thoughts are the same as behavior. They are from a neurologic point of view, but not from an external result point of view. In other words I can have an anxiety attack as a result of my thoughts and beliefs, but in fact the situation out there usually has many more options, than "my" restricted definition of it. In other words there is a sense of independence that we can create from our tacit assumptions which have created a false isomorphism between the inside and outside. I use a method called flip/flop which entails moving from emotion to thought to action and back again in an almost random fashion.

An important assumption underlying our polytheistic method is that feelings of inadequacy are signs that a person is still alive and has the potential to create a larger and more enjoyable CM. These feelings are not negative, but simply statements that the world is unpredictable, and will always remain so. Like the monotheism of religion or Hitler we can try to force a limited CM on the worlds in order to reduce our sense of uneasiness. However the result of this is obvious. Us 0 Lawyers 46

Rather than feeling bad about our feelings of inadequacy we begin to realize that it is a sign of the unknown in life. It simply means that you are preparing to feel open to the unknown and that you can function without having to predict or create the future compulsively. Being open to discovery and newness always implies the feeling of inadequacy which is quite different from **being** inadequate or worthless.

Many of us spend much of our lives trying to control or prevent the unexpected. Individuals who take on challenges inherently accept the possibility of failure and their feelings of doubt and inadequacy. However, many of us have been taught that we need to build a totally organized and predictable world in order for us to Be Ok.

THE NEW MYTH OF BROTHER/SISTER POLYTHEISM

According to some, the Isis, mother, monotheistic matriarchy, was replaced by the father, monotheistic Osiris patriarchy. Whether true or false, the image here is one of mono-mania, myopia and finally exhaustion. Not only should patriarchy and matriarchy die, but so should its underlying idea of monotheism.
Us 093 Lawyers 0.

The modern female cult supports the notion of the Great Mother consciousness replacing the sagging Father cult. However, I see no benefit in returning to a monotheistic matriarchy. I hold that the notion of monotheism, whether male or female is dead.

In one myth of the coming New Age, we are told that Horus, the Hawk Headed God will reign. I do not believe that his job is to rule but to simply Undo what has preceeded him. He is simply one of the pantheon of Gods who will usher in the era of brother/sister polytheism. In other words the human race may have grown up enough to try a brother/sister religions replacing the monotheism of the Mother/Father religions of the past 5000 years. I believe that the implications of a brother/sister polytheism will allow us to free ourselves from the domination of both Mother and Father security and worship. No longer will we lose our individuality, to the male/violent structure of blind slavery to dumb authority. We will become diverse in the sense of being authoritative, serving truths and data and not simply the One God-Brain. This is my vision and to its end I have dedicated my life.

Sister/Brother will manifest themselves in new and divergent fashions, each and both modifying our visions of ourselves and the world. However, it appears to me that Horus the Hawk—Headed God must first have his say. That is, his violence is really in the service of a euthanasia, a mercy killing of not only Father and Mother, but of MONOTHEISM itself.

MOVING ON

Saying Good-Bye to Undoing for now is both sad and hopeful. As we are Undone, we must begin to ask — What Next? This answer is Making Life Work. When we are Undone it is time to re-organize our humaness, our unique irreplacable responses to life. Now imperfect again, we are free to use our imperfection as an opportunity to change and grow with compassion and severity, with hearts and minds, becoming each Brothers/Sisters to all.

Conclusion: There is no need to keep score!

REACHING HYATT CONSCIOUSNESS

Many individuals have contacted Falcon Press asking if Dr. Hyatt has come out of his 8 years of seclusion. The answer is yes. Not only has he returned to civilization, he is now available for lectures.

More importantly he is ready and able to work with individuals and groups at his new Making Life Work Center in California. For those who wish to reach him, please write to Dr. C.S. Hyatt, c/o Falcon Press 2210 Wilshire Blvd. Suite 295 Santa Monica, Ca. 90403. Or call for an appointment at 213-821-3540

Thank You,
Nick Tharcher

UNDOING YOURSELF
AN AFTERWORD:
By Antero Alli

UNDOING YOURSELF is written with the force of a "madman" and the precision of a brain surgeon, so it goes without saying that this is a dangerous book. It is dangerous because it is ALIVE and anything truly alive is a threat to THE UNLIVING, who are now forming the FUTURE FURNITURE BUYERS of AMERICA in order to render contagious the psychic disease of Terminal Complacency. In this sense, Dr. Hyatt has entered the Front Lines as an exterminating agent in the newest, most advanced Germ Warfare of all. . .battling the virus of the rapidly expanding fundamentalist mentality. This lurid, insidious plague drifts through the very air we breathe. . .changing forms. . .from the insipid New Age Cosmic Fu Foo Movement to the Last Gasp Desperation of the Moral Majority and on into the Hard, Cold World of Government-funded Science Projects. Quite fortunately, for all concerned, Hyatt's secret weapon is not so secret at all. . .it's funny. His artillery of blistering humor is often enough to blow your ship right out of the water.

Having spent considerable time with Dr. Hyatt personally, I can attest to several things. . .he is absolutely "crazed". He is also brilliant and one of the more compassionate men I've met. His book, Undoing Yourself, is a secret neurological autobiography as it effectively transmits his essence in real life. He writes as he speaks and he speaks as he thinks. He also does what he says. That alone is worth the price of Admission into The Hyatt Theatre. Some people around here think he's one of the notorious Secret Chiefs, whose astral prowess has enabled him to walk through walls and see what goes on behind closed doors. I don't know what to think, so, I don't. Instead, when I want a good dose of UNDOING MYSELF. . .I visit Dr. Hyatt for a "shock treatment". For those who have not found his office, his number has been unlisted until now for some Very Good Reasons. This is no longer a problem since he is now open to Undoing Everyone. This book should not be sold without a prescription from your local shaman priest and/or a written note from your mother. Should you be out of touch with either one, order it direct from Falcon Press because not every bookstore will carry it. WHY? (Reread the first two sentences of the first paragraph on this page.)

UNDOING is Hyatt's forte. The presentation of this book has been strategically executed to dis-man-tle your pretenses, piss you off and direct you down the hall to the Laboratory. I found his Chakra Therapy treatment especially helpful to my own growing knowledge in the Art of Falling Apart, (See my book Angel Tech, Falcon Press) an indispensible skill for "creative types" learning to take responsibility for their own destruction. As Greg Hill put it in his underground classic, PRINCIPIA DISCORDIA (paraphrased), "There are two forms of destruction: 1) Destructive Destruction and 2) Creative Destruction." As a Quick-Decay Artist, I prefer the latter style of personal dissolution during times of excessive rigidity often resulting from abnormal self-emphasis. It seems that highly creative individuals tend to calcify quicker than Homo Normalis due to ther penchant for falling in love with their self-created structures. Unless we are as awake as children, we forget we were pretending and become the things we imagine. . .statues. . .frozen parodies of who we used to be. "Dr. Hyatt to the operating room. . .Dr. Hyatt. . ."

I recommend this book to Children Everywhere. . .the Child Within and those who have not slipped into the Great Unwashed Tub of Runny Shit. These people are the Hope of the West. I suggest this book to people with Drug Problems (alcohol, downers, uppers) as an alternative route to killing themselves. You may die laughing but no matter how you look at it, birth hurts and we must die to be reborn. So choose your poison mate! I reluctantly refer this book to the vast majority currently suffering from Terminal Mellowness, be it the New Age Human Potentialists or the Languid, Pot-Bellied Televisionaries. . use this book as a firecracker suppository, light the fuse and bend over. I do not recommend, suggest or refer this book to anybody else. . .it's too dangerous and who's going to clean up the mess?

"Can I Go Now, Dr. Hyatt?"
"OK Antero, don't fly too close to the sun."

Antero Alli
Author-ANGEL TECH
Boulder Colorado

CYBER—SHAMANS
THE NEW WAVE

I have been asked over and over again, "what is the wave of the future?" My answer has been, "wait, it will emerge in its own good time." As of yesterday the vision appeared, and the 'name' which came is **Cyber-Shaman**. Now! What is a **Cyber-Shaman?**

From the Greek, CYBER is steerman, or pilot. More modern definitions flow from the field of cybernetics, "the control and communication in machines and organisms." The key here is 'control' and 'steerman'. Also we have the implication of engineering, a pragmatic and applied 'science', whose focus is functional, observable and 'useful'.

The word **Shaman** denotes a magician, a wizard, a medicine man. It relates to the control of 'spirits', 'demons', through the medium of the priest-craft (neural know how).

If we substitute neural for spirits and demons, we may conclude that the **Cyber-Shaman** is a pilot-neural-engineer. What does this mean? I will explain.

First, a thought, an image, etc. can create a similar and sometimes identical neural-physiological reaction, as a "real event." For clarity sake and for historical purposes a "real event" simply means an "out-there event." (An In-There Event is a phrase for a brain-mind event). For example an image of a car hitting you, can create a similar physiological reaction, as the "out there" event of a car hitting you. In fact some people can and do kill themselves by creating (In-there) emergency events. This has been historically known as **Voodoo Death**. This fact alone demonstrates the potential power of our psycho-neural-biology and relates well to the "need" for isomorphism.

As a onetime psychotherapist, most of my patients were not **Cyber-Shamans** but neural passengers. Their error lay in the fact that they were "unconsciously" creating emergency events, that is real neural-physiological reactions, and then in devious ways attempting to get the "out there" to verify and vibrate to their (in-there) creations. In other words they were trying to get the car to hit them. An interesting form of **Voodoo?**

My role was to stop them from creating "bogus" neural-physiological reactions and to prevent them from getting "out there" to match their neural-creations.

Using various techniques ranging from body-work, pleading, hypnosis, etc. I was able to deflect the process. However, what I noted was that they still continued creating new neural-events which they tried to match, most often unsuccessfully, with "out-there". Observering so-called "normal" people I noticed the same process. Beliefs, hopes, ideas, create neural-physiological reactions. I have now concluded that we are all potential **Cyber-Shamans**, and what is missing is that **most do not** know this, nor **do most** have the technology to "create" the desired neural-physiological reactions, and then the know-how to mold the "out there" to match.

As an outgrowth of Dr. Timothy Leary's pioneering work in Cyber-psychology, interactive software and films, and my work in magical practices, hypnosis, and body therapy, we are jointly developing a series of books and Cyber-training centers. The Cyber-Centers will focus on how to use your Head, Heart, Emotions and Sexual Energies to become your own Pilot and Navigator, a **Cyber-Shaman.**